THE SCIENCE FACT BOOK FOR CHILDREN

FASCINATING SCIENCE AND NATURE FACTS TO INSPIRE CURIOSITY AND FAMILY FUN

MARTIN VILLORIA

© **Copyright 2024 Martin U. Villoria - All rights reserved.**

The content within this book may not be reproduced, duplicated, or transmitted without direct written permission from the author or the publisher.

Under no circumstances will any blame or legal responsibility be held against the publisher, or author, for any damages, reparation, or monetary loss due to the information contained within this book. Either directly or indirectly. You are responsible for your own choices, actions, and results.

Legal Notice:

This book is copyright-protected. This book is only for personal use. You cannot amend, distribute, sell, use, quote, or paraphrase any part, of the content within this book, without the consent of the author or publisher.

Disclaimer Notice:

Please note the information contained within this document is for educational and entertainment purposes only. All effort has been expended to present accurate, up-to-date, and reliable, complete information. No warranties of any kind are declared or implied. Readers acknowledge that the author is not engaging in the rendering of legal, financial, medical or professional advice. The content within this book has been derived from various sources. Please consult a licensed professional before attempting any techniques outlined in this book.

By reading this document, the reader agrees that under no circumstances is the author responsible for any losses, direct or indirect, which are incurred as a result of the use of the information contained within this document, including, but not limited to, — errors, omissions, or inaccuracies.

CONTENTS

Introduction	5
1. MARVELS OF ROBOTICS AND ENGINEERING	9
The Basics of Robotics: How Robots Work	10
The Evolution of Computers	13
Engineering Bridges: Balancing Forces	17
The Science of Flight: How Airplanes Fly	21
Renewable Energy: Powering the Future	25
Engineering Disasters: Lessons from Failure	29
2. INCREDIBLE BIOLOGY AND LIFE SCIENCES	33
Animal Superpowers: Unique Adaptations in Nature	33
The Science of Animal Communication	37
The Mysteries of Bioluminescent Creatures	40
How Plants "Eat" Sunlight: Photosynthesis Explained	43
The Amazing World of Microorganisms	46
DNA: The Blueprint of Life	50
3. WONDERS OF ASTRONOMY AND SPACE SCIENCE	53
The Solar System: Our Cosmic Neighborhood	54
The Moon: Earth's Celestial Companion	59
Planets Beyond Our Solar System	63
The Life Cycle of Stars	67
The Mysteries of Black Holes	70
Exploring the Milky Way Galaxy	73
4. HUMAN BODY AND HEALTH	77
The Human Brain: Our Body's Control Center	78
The Circulatory System: Our Body's Highway	81
The Digestive System: From Food to Fuel	83
How Our Immune System Fights Germs	87
The Skeletal System: Our Body's Framework	89
The Science of Sleep: Why We Need It	92

5. PHYSICS IN EVERYDAY LIFE   99
   Gravity: Why We Don't Float Away   99
   Simple Machines: Making Work Easier   102
   Magnetism: Invisible Forces at Work   105
   The Basics of Electricity: Powering Our World   108
   The Science of Sound: How We Hear   113
   Light and Optics: How We See   115

6. CHEMISTRY AROUND US   119
   Atoms and Molecules: The Building Blocks of Matter   119
   The Periodic Table: Organizing the Elements   122
   Chemical Reactions: How Substances Change   125
   Acids and Bases: The Science of pH   128
   Polymers: The Science of Plastics   131
   The Chemistry of Cooking: How Heat Transforms Food   134

7. EARTH SCIENCE AND GEOLOGY UNCOVERED   139
   Volcanoes: Earth's Fiery Mountains   139
   Earthquakes: When the Ground Shakes   143
   The Rock Cycle: How Rocks Transform   145
   Glaciers: Earth's Ice Sculptors   148
   Fossils: Clues to Earth's Past   152
   The Water Cycle: From Rain to Rivers   155

Conclusion   159

BONUS CHAPTER: FAMILY QUIZ & FUN FACTS   165
   Multiple-Choice Questions   166
   True or False—Quiz   173
   A summary of fun facts and tidbits   176

References   181

INTRODUCTION

Did you know that honey never spoils? Archaeologists have found honey pots in ancient Egyptian tombs that are over 3,000 years old and still perfectly edible. This fascinating fact is just one of the many wonders of science that we will uncover together in this book. Science is full of surprises and is all around us, waiting to be discovered.

Why is understanding **science** so important for children? Science helps us make sense of the **world around us**. It teaches us how things work and why they happen. It encourages **critical thinking** and **problem-solving skills**. Most importantly, science fosters a **sense of wonder** and curiosity that can last a **lifetime**. Children who understand science are better equipped to navigate the world and make **informed decisions**.

Welcome to *The Science Fact Book for Children: Fascinating Science and Nature Facts to Inspire Curiosity and Family Fun*. This book is a treasure trove of amazing facts and stories from various fields of science. It is designed primarily to be a possible shared experience for families. It is an opportunity for parents and children to learn together, sparking interesting conversations and shared discoveries. Whether reading at home or listening to the audio version during a road trip, this book transforms learning moments into quality family time. Hence, this book differs from others that discuss similar topics. It follows a narrative essay format, which differs from typical quiz-type fact compilations or textbook-style publications. This approach allows you to immerse yourself in the text and let your imagination do the rest. While the illustrations used in this book enhance the visual experience, the real magic happens in your mind as you read and visualize the concepts. Relatable examples and practical references to everyday observations make science more tangible. There are plenty of good-quality science introduction books around that have numerous illustrations, graphs, and pictures. However, I found myself too often being interrupted when flowing through the main text and constantly being forced to look at diagrams, photos, and illustrations. Sometimes, I just wanted to read (or listen to audiobooks) and do the picture search on my own with my phone, but later, when I had finished reading about a topic. This book works without the provided illustrations. Still, I have added them to give some visual experience.

Allow me to introduce myself. I am Martin Villoria, a father and Mechanical Engineer. I worked as a Chief Technology Officer for a publicly traded company and served as a Navy Officer on submarines. When not working or writing a book, you will find me biking or hiking with my family. I am also a private pilot and may spend some nights studying astronomy with my telescope. My life has been deeply rooted in curiosity, exploration, and discovery. Finally, my passion for science and nature drives me to make complex scientific concepts accessible to children and their parents.

Which topics are covered in this book? It is structured to cover a wide range of scientific fields. We will explore the wonders of **Robotics and Engineering**, the intricacies of **Biology and Life Sciences**, the mysteries of **Astronomy and Space Science**, the complexities of the **Human Body and Health**, the principles of **Physics**, the marvels of **Chemistry**, and the dynamics of **Earth Science and Geology**. In each chapter, I hand-picked six exciting topics, and typically, each one ends with fun facts or inspirations for observations, encouraging you to explore the world around you. The final chapter is a quiz designed to test your knowledge and promote family interaction and fun.

So, I invite you to dive into this book with an open mind and a curious spirit. Let's discover the fascinating world of science together. Let's smile, learn, and be amazed by the universe's wonders. This book promises to entertain and educate, making complex science topics simple and understandable with no formula used. Join us on this journey, and let your curiosity lead the way.

The adventure awaits.

CHAPTER ONE
MARVELS OF ROBOTICS AND ENGINEERING

Have you ever wondered how a robot can perform precise tasks or how a plane stays in the sky despite its weight? These incredible feats result from **Robotics and Engineering**—fields where science and creativity come together to solve complex problems. In this chapter, we'll explore the **Basics of Robotics**, from how robots move to the clever programming that guides them. We'll journey through the **Evolution of Computers**, the brains behind much of today's technology, and dive into **Bridge Engineering**, where balancing forces is vital to keeping massive structures standing. Ever wonder how airplanes take flight? We'll uncover the **Science of Flight** and look into **Renewable Energy**, exploring new systems aiming to power a more sustainable future. Lastly, we'll learn valuable lessons from **Engineering Disasters**, showing that sometimes failure is the first step toward innovation.

THE BASICS OF ROBOTICS: HOW ROBOTS WORK

Robots are, in many ways, mechanical images of living creatures. Like humans, they have bodies that move, senses that detect their surroundings, brains that make decisions, and power sources that keep them going. At the heart of every robot is a combination of these fundamental components: sensors, actuators, controllers, and a power supply. Each part plays a critical role in making the robot function.

Sensors are the robot's eyes and ears, allowing it to detect and interpret information from its environment. These can include cameras that capture visual data, ultrasonic sensors that measure distance using sound waves, and touch sensors that detect physical contact. For instance, your robot vacuum uses a combination of cameras and ultrasonic sensors to navigate your home and avoid obstacles, and they prevent it from tumbling down the stairs.

Actuators are the robot's muscles, responsible for moving its parts. These can be motors that rotate wheels or arms, hydraulic pistons that provide powerful linear motion, or even servos that offer precise control over angles and positions. Imagine a robotic arm in a factory picking up a car part and placing it on an assembly line. The actuators in that arm make the precise, repetitive motions possible.

Controllers are like the robot's brain, processing sensor information and sending commands to the actuators. This is typically done through a computer or microcontroller that runs software programs, often written—typically by humans—in coding languages like Python or C++. The controller decides the robot's actions based on the data it receives. For example, suppose a robotic vacuum's sensors detect a wall. In that case, the controller processes this information and commands the actuators to change direction.

The **power supply** is the robot's energy source, without which none of the other components can function. This could be a battery, solar cells, or an electrical outlet. The type of power supply chosen depends on the robot's application and the amount of power it needs. A small household robot might use rechargeable batteries, while an industrial robot could be plugged into the mains electricity.

Robots come in many shapes and sizes, each designed for specific tasks. **Industrial robots**, for example, are commonly found in manufacturing plants, where they automate repetitive tasks like welding, painting, and assembling parts. These robots increase efficiency and precision, significantly reducing the margin of human error.

Medical robots assist in surgeries, providing doctors with enhanced precision and control, especially in minimally invasive procedures. These robots can also be used in patient care, lifting and transporting patients, or delivering medication.

Service robots are becoming more common in our daily lives. They can perform household tasks like vacuuming, mowing the lawn, or even acting as personal assistants. Some service robots are designed for customer service, such as those in hotels or restaurants that can check you in or deliver your meal.

Exploration robots take on the challenges humans cannot, venturing into space, underwater, and moving into disaster zones. NASA's Mars rovers, for example, explore the Martian surface, conducting experiments and sending data back to Earth.

Programming is what brings robots to life, allowing them to perform tasks autonomously or under human control. Coding languages like Python and C++ are often used to write, hence, "to program," the software that runs on the robot's controller. Such programs are typically made of algorithms, which often are essential to such programs, providing step-by-step instructions for solving problems or completing tasks, making them indispensable in programming robots. These algorithms can be simple or highly complex, depending on what the robot needs to do. Robots can be autonomous, making decisions on their own based on their programming and sensor data, or they can be remote-controlled, operated by a human using a joystick or computer interface. We will get back to computers and software in the next sub-chapter.

MARVELS OF ROBOTICS AND ENGINEERING   13

You can observe robots in action in various settings. In everyday life, you might see robotic devices like automated checkout systems at grocery stores, robotic vacuum cleaners in homes, or even simple robotic toys. Take a moment to reflect on the inputs these robots have to process and the controls they must have to perform their tasks. You can also find videos or virtual tours online, where industrial robots are shown in action. Many manufacturing companies and educational websites offer behind-the-scenes looks at how robots are used in production lines.

Robotics is a field teeming with innovation and possibilities. As explained earlier, it combines skills from different engineering fields, building on science fundamentals. As you explore this whole chapter, you'll understand typical engineering fields better. These fields require knowledge of sciences from different domains, as do the ones in the other main chapters of this book.

Finally, whether you observe a robot vacuuming your living room or watch a Mars rover send back images from another planet, you're witnessing the marvel of robotics and engineering in action.

THE EVOLUTION OF COMPUTERS

Imagine a world where complex calculations took long periods, like days or weeks, and the word "computer" referred to a person, not a machine. That was the reality not too long ago. The word "Computer" used to be a **job title** for someone who performs calculations as a profession for a living.

The history of computers as we know them today is a fascinating tale of innovation and ingenuity that has transformed our lives in countless ways. It all began with early mechanical computers like the **abacus**, a simple yet powerful instrument for mathematical calculations like summing and subtracting by moving beads on bars.

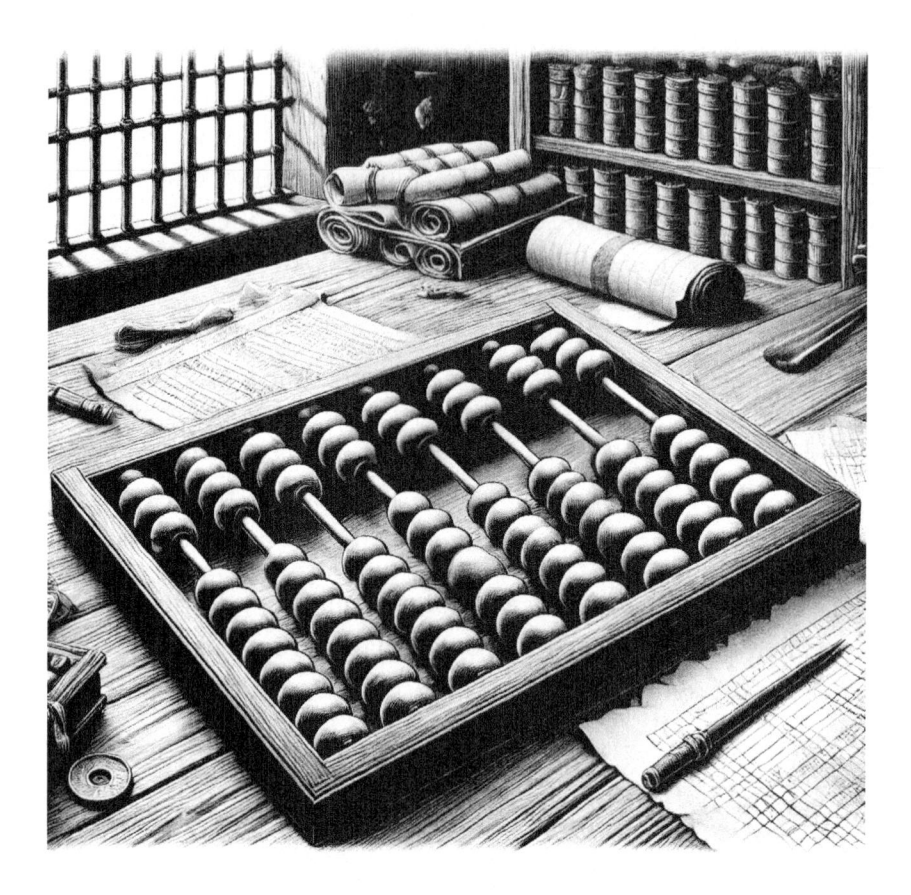

Fast forward to the 19th century, and we meet Charles Babbage, the father of the computer. His invention, the **Analytical Engine**, was a marvel of its time, a pure mechanical device capable of performing complex calculations. As you can imagine from its name, the "analytical engine mill," the design is far different from today's computers, consisting of gears, wheels, axles, and cages. Though it was never completed, Babbage's vision laid the groundwork for future developments and—by the way—did already conceptually contain most of the principal elements of modern computers, which we will discuss later.

The first electronic computers emerged in the mid-20th century, marking a significant leap forward. Built in 1945, the ENIAC (**Electronic Numerical Integrator and Computer**) was a behemoth that occupied an entire room and used thousands of vacuum tubes. It could perform calculations at unprecedented speeds, revolutionizing fields like cryptography and weather forecasting. Shortly after, the UNIVAC (Universal Automatic Computer) became the first commercially available computer, bringing computing power to businesses and government agencies.

The 1980s saw the rise of **personal computers**, making technology accessible to the masses. Companies like Apple and IBM introduced machines that could fit on a desk, forever changing how we work, learn, and play. The Apple Macintosh, with its user-friendly interface, set the standard for personal computing. At the same time, IBM's PCs became the backbone of business operations worldwide. These machines brought computing power into homes, schools, and offices, democratizing access to information and tools.

Today, modern computing has transformed beyond recognition. We carry **smartphones** in our pockets and **tablets** in our bags while accessing cloud computing services that store and process data remotely. These devices are more powerful than the early mainframes, yet they fit in the palm of our hands. **Cloud computing** allows us to access information and applications from anywhere, enabling remote work, online learning, and seamless collaboration.

When we explore the hardware of a typical computer, we'll uncover a set of essential components that work together. Let's think first in general terms of what a computer has to be able to do. We can come up with the following general elements: a brain able to compute, short-term and long-term memory, and ways to get data in and out. Accordingly, if we dissect a modern-day computer, we would find the following components or types of blocks.

The **Central Processing Unit (CPU)**, often called the computer's brain, is at the heart of almost every computer. The CPU performs calculations and executes instructions, driving every operation.

Memory, or RAM (Random Access Memory), temporarily stores data the CPU needs to access quickly. Unlike storage devices, RAM is volatile, meaning it loses data when the computer is turned off.

Long-term **storage**, such as hard drives and solid-state drives (SSDs), provides long-term data retention, holding everything from operating systems to personal files.

Input/output devices like keyboards, mice, and monitors allow us to interact with the computer, entering data and receiving feedback.

The impact of computers on society is profound. In communication, they've revolutionized how we connect with others. Email replaced snail mail, social media brought people together across continents, and video calls made face-to-face conversations possible from afar. Education and work have also transformed. Online learning platforms offer courses on virtually any subject; digital textbooks provide interactive content, and remote work has become a norm, facilitated by collaboration tools and automation technologies.

Entertainment has been equally revolutionized. Video games have evolved into immersive experiences, streaming services provide endless content at our fingertips, and social media platforms offer new ways to share and consume information. **Artificial Intelligence (AI)** is another frontier that is growing in usage in professional life. AI algorithms power everything from recommendation engines on many digital platforms we use today to autonomous vehicles and complex data analysis in healthcare. In the next 10–20 years, AI could revolutionize industries, create new job opportunities, and introduce ethical considerations about automation and decision-making.

Constructing a simple circuit using a breadboard and basic components like resistors, LEDs, and a power source can be an enlightening, hands-on learning experience. Many kits and video instructions are available on the web for this activity, which teaches the fundamentals of electronics and how computers process signals.

Another activity to explore the computing field is to try basic coding with beginner-friendly tools like Scratch or Python. These platforms are great entry points and offer free resources and tutorials, making it easy to start programming and understand the logic behind software development. You will find a link with a simple example in the Bibliography.

ENGINEERING BRIDGES: BALANCING FORCES

Bridges, those majestic structures connecting distant shores, are marvels of engineering. You may think, bridges, really? Yes, bridges. While we explore these a bit, you will see some of the many considerations they incorporate. Bridges balance opposing forces to stay upright and strong. Compression, tension, and load distribution are critical forces in bridge engineering.

Compression is a force that pushes inward, like when you squeeze a spring. In a bridge, compression acts on the deck and support pillars, pressing them together.

Tension, on the other hand, pulls outward, similar to stretching a rubber band. It acts on the cables and beams, pulling them apart.

Load distribution is the art of spreading weight evenly across the structure, ensuring no single point bears too much stress.

Civil engineers must master these principles. As a start, they need to investigate and understand how to size different loads, which can be, of course, derived from what will be on the future bridge itself, like cars, trucks, and so on, but also its own future weight and risk of external forces as earthquake risk areas. Another step is to choose suitable materials based on their properties and use calculations and simulations to ensure the bridge can handle the forces it will encounter. Drawing up detailed plans requires knowledge of physics, materials science, and structural analysis. Yet, the result is deeply satisfying for the performing engineer. There's immense pride in seeing a bridge stand tall, knowing it started as a sketch on paper and now connects people and places. While I did not design bridges, I did design turbomachines. I remember, as it was today, the strong enrichment feeling I had when seeing components being manufactured and then assembled into an entire machine, which I calculated and designed from a blank sheet of paper months earlier. Finally, it was about calculating and sketching through many iterations—yet something had been created that did not exist before.

Going back to our bridges, we can find different types:

Beam bridges, the simplest and most cost-effective, rely on horizontal beams supported at each end. Think of a plank laid across a stream.

Arch bridges, like the beautiful stone bridges of old times, use curved arches to distribute weight through compression. The shape directs the force down into the supports at each end, making them strong and aesthetically pleasing.

Suspension bridges, such as the iconic Golden Gate Bridge in San Francisco, US, use cables suspended from towers to hold up the bridge deck. These cables handle tension while the towers bear the compression.

Cable-stayed bridges, like the sleek Millau Viaduct in France, use cables directly connected to towers to support the bridge deck, offering a modern and efficient design.

Famous bridges around the world illustrate the incredible feats of engineering involved. With its striking orange hue and sweeping curves, the Golden Gate Bridge spans the Golden Gate Strait, connecting San Francisco to Marin County. It's a testament to the power of suspension design, with its main cables stretching over 7,000 feet. Tower Bridge in London is both a bascule and suspension bridge, allowing it to open for passing ships. Its Victorian Gothic style makes it one of the most recognizable bridges in the world. The Millau Viaduct, soaring over the Tarn River Valley in France, is the tallest bridge in the world, with its highest tower reaching 1,125 feet. Its cable-stayed design is not only efficient but also stunningly graceful.

To truly appreciate these engineering marvels, consider organizing a family outing to observe different types of bridges in your area or during a trip. Focus on identifying designs such as beam, arch, suspension, and cable-stayed bridges. Notice how each type handles the forces of compression and tension. A simple way to imagine how forces transmit through the structure is the method of exaggerated loads. Think of a massively heavy object like a monstrous truck or tank in the middle of the bridge. Are there simple pillars or also cables in use? Which of the components are loaded by compression, and which by tension? Will you likely observe that components facing compression might be concrete while tensioned components are made of steel?

Another activity is to visit a pedestrian footbridge and observe how it reacts to pedestrians' weight. Look for visible signs of stress or strain as people walk across or when groups gather in one spot. Please pay attention to design features such as supports, trusses, or arches and how they distribute the weight.

Understanding bridge engineering is more than just learning about forces and materials. It's about seeing the practical application of science and the beauty of human ingenuity. Engineers take immense pride in their creations, knowing they've built something that serves a vital purpose and stands as a testament to their skills and creativity. Workers have put their power and skills into building them, maybe by using heavy machines. Robots may have been used to produce steel components during the manufacturing phases.

The next time you cross a bridge, take a moment to appreciate the thought and effort that went into making it strong, safe, and enduring.

THE SCIENCE OF FLIGHT: HOW AIRPLANES FLY

Imagine you're at the airport, watching a massive airplane lift off the ground and soar into the sky. It seems almost magical, but it's all about mastering the principles of flight.

The history of flight is a tale of human ingenuity and persistence. The modern airplanes started with the Wright brothers, who made history in 1903 with the first powered flight in Kitty Hawk, North Carolina, in the United States. Their aircraft, the Wright Flyer, flew for just 12 seconds, but it marked the beginning of aviation. The development of jet engines in the following decades revolutionized air travel, allowing aircraft to fly faster, higher, and more efficiently. Frank Whittle in the UK and Hans von Ohain in

Germany are credited with independently developing the first jet engines during the late 1930s and early 1940s. Modern aircraft have come a long way since then, incorporating advanced materials, computer systems, and aerodynamic designs. Today's airplanes are marvels of technology, capable of easily crossing continents and oceans.

But let's take the time to step into the shoes of a scientist and analyze the loads acting. Four main forces are involved: lift, thrust, drag, and weight.

Lift is the force that pulls the airplane upward, generated by the wings. When air flows over and under the wings, it creates a pressure difference, lifting the plane.

The engines provide **thrust**, propelling the airplane forward. Jet engines or propellers push air backward, producing the forward motion needed to take off.

Drag is the resistance the airplane encounters as it moves through the air, opposing thrust. The smoother and more aerodynamic the shape, the less drag it experiences.

Weight, the force of gravity, pulls the airplane down. We will encounter gravity in several chapters and learn more about it in the physics section. In simple terms, gravity forces all objects to the ground.

Balancing all these forces is critical to achieving and maintaining flight.

MARVELS OF ROBOTICS AND ENGINEERING 23

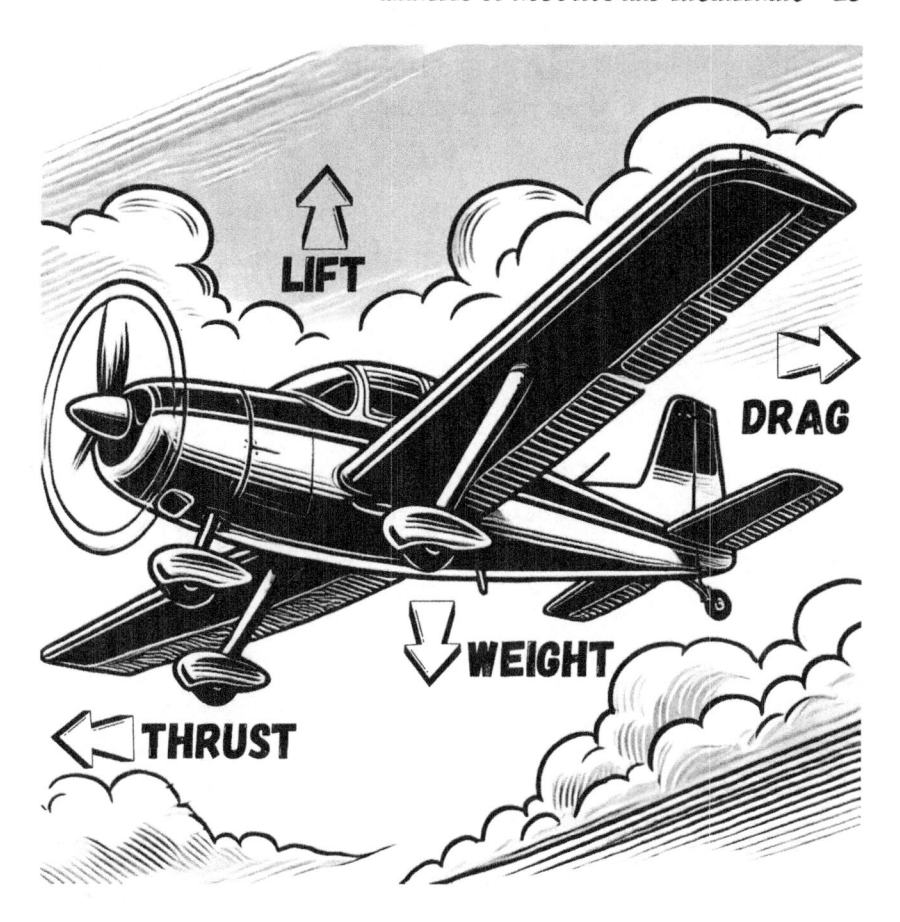

Now, let's break down the parts of an airplane and their functions.

The **wings** are perhaps the most critical component in creating lift. Shaped like an airfoil, they have a curved upper surface and a flatter lower surface, allowing air to flow faster over the top than the bottom. This difference in speed generates lift.

The **fuselage** is the main body of the aircraft, housing the cockpit, passengers, and cargo. It's designed to be aerodynamic, reducing drag.

Engines, whether jet engines or propellers, provide the thrust to propel the plane forward. Located under the wings or at the rear, they play a crucial role in achieving takeoff and maintaining speed.

The **tail**, or empennage, helps stabilize and control the aircraft. It consists of the horizontal stabilizer, which controls pitch, and the vertical stabilizer, which controls yaw.

These components work together to ensure the airplane flies smoothly and responds to pilot inputs.

Elaborating on the size of the four load types and how they are being calculated and influenced reflects the scientific approach of an engineer who, in this case, would be designing a new plane and its components mentioned earlier.

Naturally, much more detailed design principles, calculations, software simulations, and manufacturing steps are required to design airplanes. But everything boils down to the principles we discussed earlier when you got the first lesson of an aerodynamic engineering course…

For a hands-on learning experience, visit an airport, airfield, or model plane park to observe airplanes as they take off and land. Notice and pay attention to how they accelerate on the runway, gaining the speed needed for lift-off. Or watch how they gradually descend for landing. Observe the wings, in particular the **flaps**. Flaps look like movable panels on the trailing edge of the wings that can be moved or turned during takeoff and landing to **increase lift and drag**. They help the plane take off at lower speeds and provide more control during landing. Understanding their role and observing their use can provide practical insights into flight mechanics.

Another engaging activity is to observe birds in flight. Spend time in a natural setting, watching different birds as they take off, fly, and land. Notice how small birds, like sparrows, take off quickly and maneuver easily, while larger birds, like eagles, take longer to lift off but glide gracefully once airborne. Please pay attention to their wing movements. Small birds often flap rapidly, while larger birds may glide or hover. Compare these behaviors with how airplanes maneuver. Birds are natural aviators, and their flight mechanics closely resemble aircraft. By observing them, you can gain a deeper appreciation of the principles of flight—which used to be one of the oldest dreams humans have had. Today, it is considered normal thanks to the science and engineering involved.

RENEWABLE ENERGY: POWERING THE FUTURE

Every day, we rely on energy to power almost everything in our lives—from the lights in our homes to the cars we drive and even the machines that help us work and play. When you flip a switch, charge your phone, or ride the bus, you use energy in different forms, like electricity and fuel. We might not always see it, but energy constantly flows around us, making our modern world possible. The sources of the various types of energy we use daily are different, and some of them are limited as we use them today. Imagine a world where humanity's use of energy is not depleting the planet's resources or polluting the environment. This is the promise of renewable energy, a field gaining momentum and reshaping our future. Renewable energy sources naturally replenish themselves over time, unlike non-renewable sources such as oil, natural gas, and coal, which are limited and cause significant environmental harm. Renewables offer a sustainable way to power our lives and reduce greenhouse gas emissions. Let's discuss the most common ones.

Firstly, **solar energy** harnesses the power of the Sun, the most abundant energy source available. Photovoltaic cells built into solar panels convert electricity from sunlight. This technology can be used on a small scale, like rooftop panels on homes, or on a large scale in solar farms that generate electricity for thousands of homes. One of the most appealing aspects of solar energy is its accessibility. Almost anyone with sufficient sunlight can install solar panels and start generating electricity, reducing both their reliance on the grid and their carbon footprint.

Wind energy generates electricity by capturing the kinetic energy of moving air with turbines. Wind farms, often situated in open plains or offshore, have numerous wind turbines working together. The turbine blades catch the wind, spinning a generator that produces electricity. Wind energy can provide significant amounts of power, especially in areas with consistent wind patterns. The visual of wind turbines dotting the landscape is becoming increasingly common. It serves as a symbol of our transition to cleaner energy.

Hydropower generates electricity by converting the energy of flowing water. Dams are commonly used to create reservoirs, where, once released, the stored water flows through turbines, producing electricity. Hydropower has been a reliable energy source for decades. It is particularly effective in regions with large rivers or significant rainfall, sometimes in mountainous terrain offering naturally elevated reservoirs. While building dams can have environmental impacts, modern designs aim to minimize these effects and integrate with local ecosystems.

Geothermal energy taps into the Earth's internal heat, using steam or hot water from underground reservoirs to generate electricity or provide direct heating. This energy source is especially effective in regions with volcanic activity or geothermal hotspots. Geothermal plants have a small land footprint and can operate continuously, providing a stable power supply with minimal environmental impact.

Other energy sources not considered renewable, such as nuclear power and fossil fuels, play significant roles in our current energy landscape. Nuclear power generates electricity through nuclear fission, splitting atoms to release energy. It produces minimal greenhouse gases but raises concerns about radioactive waste and safety. However, it remains one alternative to provide base loads in the future. Fossil fuels like oil, coal, and natural gas are abundant and energy-dense but contribute heavily to carbon emissions and environmental degradation. While these sources are not renewable, they have historically provided the bulk of our energy needs and continue to do so as we transition to greener alternatives.

The benefits of renewable energy are numerous. They enhance energy independence, reducing reliance on imported fuels and increasing energy security. However, there are challenges to overcome. At periods when renewable sources are not generating power, like at night for solar energy or during calm days for wind energy, storage technologies, such as batteries, are needed. Storage can also happen by converting clean sources into valuable energy carriers. One example is using solar energy to convert water into hydrogen and oxygen. Hydrogen can be used in so-called fuel cells to create electricity again while only consuming oxygen and producing water as an exhaust product. Intermittency, the variable nature of renewable sources, is another challenge that requires a flexible and resilient grid. Initial costs for renewable installations can be high, though they are decreasing as technology advances. Providing a consistent base load electricity supply remains challenging, requiring a mix of energy sources to ensure reliability.

For a hands-on experience, consider observing hydropower in natural waterways. Visit a local dam or hydroelectric plant to see how flowing water generates electricity. The common process is that the controlled water flow passes and drives the turbine wheels. The turbines, then turning, are connected to generators, which again produce electricity. Many facilities offer tours and educational programs that explain the process in detail. Reflect on how the energy of water is harnessed and the environmental considerations involved.

Another engaging activity is observing the increased application and distribution of solar panels. Look for solar installations in your community, such as on homes, schools, or public buildings. Notice the orientation and placement of the panels to maximize sunlight exposure. If possible, visit a solar farm to see a large-scale operation. Reflect on solar energy's potential in your life and how it contributes to a sustainable future.

ENGINEERING DISASTERS: LESSONS FROM FAILURE

Engineering, like any field, has its share of failures. While often tragic, these failures provide invaluable lessons that drive advancements in safety, design, and technology. Take the **Tacoma Narrows Bridge** collapse in 1940, for instance. Known as "Galloping Gertie," this suspension bridge in Washington State began to oscillate wildly in the wind just months after opening. The dramatic footage of the bridge twisting and turning before finally collapsing into Puget Sound is both mesmerizing and a stark reminder of the importance of thorough testing and understanding of aerodynamic forces and the general physics of structures.

So, what went wrong? The bridge's design failed to account for the effects of wind-induced vibrations, known as aeroelastic flutter. Essentially, the wind created a resonance that the bridge couldn't handle, leading to its collapse. The disaster prompted engineers to study aerodynamics more closely and the field of natural frequencies, leading to the development of wind tunnel testing for bridge designs. Also, evaluating, calculating, and simulating natural frequencies of structures like bridges and any buildings and machines became more of a normality during the design processes. This failure, though devastating, paved the way for safer and more reliable structures.

Another notable engineering failure was the tragic **Space Shuttle Challenger** disaster in 1986. Just 73 seconds after lift-off, the shuttle disintegrated, killing all seven crew members. The cause? A faulty O-ring seal arrangement in one of the solid rocket boosters failed to seal properly in the cold temperatures, allowing hot gases to escape and ignite the external fuel tank. In their typical shape, O-rings are simple rubber rings clamped between two components to keep the joint tight. On its own, an O-ring is a penny article you can buy at any DIY store. However, factors such as its material, how it is clamped, and how the clamped components react to pressure and temperature can be incredibly complex and require the attention of scientists and engineers. This tragedy exposed flaws in NASA's safety protocols and decision-making processes. The subsequent investigation led to significant changes in shuttle design, improved safety standards, and better communication channels within NASA.

These and many other failures highlight the importance of learning from mistakes. Testing, safety standards, and regulations are crucial in preventing future disasters. Engineers must rigorously test materials, designs, and systems to identify weaknesses. Safety standards ensure that structures and machines meet specific criteria for performance and durability. Often born from past failures, regulations provide guidelines to protect public safety and prevent similar incidents.

Redundancy and safety margins are essential components of modern engineering. Redundancy means having multiple systems in place to perform the same function, ensuring that others can take over if one fails. Safety margins involve designing systems to operate well within their maximum capacity, providing a buffer against unexpected conditions. For example, engineers use multiple cables and support systems in bridge construction to ensure stability even if one component fails. In aviation, aircraft are designed with redundant systems for critical functions like navigation, communication, and control.

Consider the development of modern airplanes. Nowadays, those incorporate advanced materials like so-called carbon-fiber-reinforced polymer, which is lighter and stronger than traditional aluminum, which was often used in the past. However, the initial design faced issues with battery fires. Engineers implemented redundant safety systems, including improved battery enclosures and monitoring systems, to prevent future incidents. These measures ensure that the overall system remains safe and operational even if one component fails.

While tragic, engineering disasters often lead to significant advancements and always provide many new findings. The learnings from the Tacoma Narrows Bridge collapse have influenced the design of modern suspension bridges, making them more resilient and safer. The Challenger disaster prompted a complete overhaul of NASA's safety protocols, ultimately making space travel safer. These failures remind us that engineering is a continuous learning, testing, and improving process.

Reflecting on these stories, it's clear that failure is not the end but a stepping stone to more outstanding achievements. Engineers must remain vigilant, continually testing and refining their designs to ensure safety and reliability. By understanding the causes of past failures, we can build a future where structures and systems are functional, resilient, and safe.

As we explore the wonders of science and engineering, remember that each success stands on the shoulders of lessons learned from failure. These stories inspire us to strive for excellence, knowing that our efforts contribute to a safer and more innovative world. Also, they show that knowledge of many different fields is essential and reflects the importance of having awareness and a background in as many science domains as possible. So, the next time you cross a bridge or watch a rocket launch, take a moment to appreciate the countless hours of testing, the rigorous safety standards, and the dedication of engineers who turn dreams into reality.

We've concluded the first chapter of our journey, which was about the actual application of many different fundamental sciences to engineering. Now, we will dive into the other science fields, starting with some fascinating wonders in biology and life sciences.

CHAPTER TWO
INCREDIBLE BIOLOGY AND LIFE SCIENCES

Welcome to the fascinating world of **Biology and Life Sciences**! In this chapter, we'll explore some of nature's most remarkable secrets, from animals with incredible **Superpowers** to their hidden methods of **Communication**. We'll dive into the glowing mysteries of **Bioluminescent Creatures**, uncover how plants "eat" sunlight through **Photosynthesis**, and look closely at the tiny **Microorganisms** that shape life on Earth. Finally, we'll unlock the incredible story of **DNA**—the blueprint that makes all living things, including you, unique! Get ready for a journey into the wonders of life all around us.

ANIMAL SUPERPOWERS: UNIQUE ADAPTATIONS IN NATURE

Adaptations result from evolution, where animals develop traits that help them survive and reproduce in their environments. One of the most common adaptations is **camouflage**, which allows animals to avoid predators or sneak up on prey by blending into their surroundings. For example, the chameleon is a master of disguise. It can change its skin color to match its environment, making it nearly invisible to predators and prey. This color change

34   THE SCIENCE FACT BOOK FOR CHILDREN

is controlled by special cells called chromatophores, which can contract or expand to show different pigments. Chameleons also use color change to communicate their mood or intentions to other chameleons.

Another remarkable adaptation is **echolocation**, used by animals like bats and dolphins to navigate and hunt in the dark. Echolocation involves emitting sound waves and listening for the echoes that bounce back from objects. This allows animals to "see" their surroundings using sound. Dolphins, for instance, produce a series of clicks that travel through the water. These clicks bounce off objects and return to the dolphin, giving it a detailed picture of what's around. This adaptation is crucial for hunting, allowing dolphins to locate fish even in murky waters or complete darkness. Maybe you have heard about sonar. That is precisely the principle being used and described here by dolphins and bats and is nothing other than the abbreviation of "Sound Navigation and Ranging."

Some other animal adaptations are downright electrifying! Take the electric eel, for example. This slippery predator uses electric shocks to stun its prey and defend itself from threats. Electric eels generate **electricity** by using specialized cells called electrocytes. When the eel is hunting or feels threatened, these cells discharge a powerful electric current, incapacitating its prey or deterring predators. This adaptation is unique and highly effective, making the electric eel a formidable hunter in its aquatic habitat.

The archerfish has a different kind of superpower. It can shoot **water jets** from its mouth to knock down insects resting on branches above the water. The fish accurately aims by adjusting the angle of its mouth and the force of the water jet. Once the insect is knocked into the water, the archerfish quickly snaps it. This adaptation allows the archerfish to expand its diet beyond aquatic prey, showcasing the incredible versatility of animal adaptations.

But why do these adaptations exist? The evolutionary purpose behind these traits is often tied to predation and defense. Animals need to catch food to survive, and they also need to avoid becoming food for other animals. Adaptations like camouflage and echolocation help animals hunt more effectively and avoid predators. For instance, the chameleon's ability to blend in with its surroundings makes it harder for predators to spot. At the same time, its color change signals aggression or submission to other chameleons, reducing the likelihood of conflict. Similarly, the electric eel's shocking adaptation ensures it has an advantage over its prey and can defend itself against larger predators.

Adaptations also help animals cope with environmental challenges. Animals have evolved unique survival traits in extreme environments, such as the deep sea or arid deserts. The mimic octopus is another fascinating example. It can imitate the appearance and movements of over 15 marine species, including venomous ones like lionfish and sea snakes. This mimicry helps the octopus avoid predators by tricking them into thinking it's something more dangerous. It's a brilliant example of adaptation through deceptive appearance.

Another incredible survivor is the tardigrade, also known as the water bear. These tiny creatures can withstand extreme temperatures, radiation, and even the vacuum of space. Tardigrades enter a state called **cryptobiosis**, where they lose almost all body water and slow their metabolism to nearly zero. In this state, they can survive harsh conditions that would be lethal to most other life forms. Tardigrades have been found in some of the most extreme environments on Earth, from the deep sea to the highest mountains, showcasing their unparalleled adaptability.

Fun facts about these fantastic creatures add to their intrigue. The mimic octopus's ability to transform into multiple species is not just for show; it's a highly effective survival strategy. Similarly, the tardigrade's resilience has earned it the title of the most indestructible creature on Earth. These unique adaptations highlight our planet's incredible diversity and ingenuity.

Understanding these animal superpowers gives us a greater appreciation for the natural world. Each adaptation, whether the chameleon's color change or the electric eel's shocking abilities, tells a story of survival and evolution, highlighting the uniqueness of the world's creation. These traits have developed over time, helping animals overcome challenges and thrive in their environments. As you explore these fascinating adaptations, remember that nature is full of surprises, and there's always something new to discover.

THE SCIENCE OF ANIMAL COMMUNICATION

Imagine how difficult life would be for humans if we couldn't see, hear, or speak—we depend on communication just as much as animals do! Whether through sound, movement, or even scents, animals have developed unique ways to connect and survive in their environments. Animal communication is like nature's secret language, where creatures use different types of signals to share important information.

Visual signals are often the most immediate and noticeable forms of communication. Animals convey messages through body language, color changes, and even light displays. For example, a peacock's magnificent tail feathers are not just for show but a visual signal to attract mates. The vibrant colors and intricate patterns signal the peacock's health and genetic quality. Similarly, many animals use body language to communicate. A dog wagging its tail, a cat arching its back, or a gorilla beating its chest are all examples of visual signals that convey emotions, intentions, or social status.

Auditory signals involve vocalizations and sounds that can travel long distances, making them practical for communication in various environments. Dolphins are masters of auditory communication, combining clicks, whistles, and body movements. These sounds serve multiple purposes, from navigating through echolocation to social interactions within their pods. Dolphins are not only masters of echolocation but also have a unique way of identifying each other. They use specific whistles that function like names, allowing them to call out to particular individuals. This ability to recognize and address each other by name is a remarkable example of social communication in the animal kingdom. Similarly, birds are well-known for their songs, which can attract mates, defend territories, or signal danger. The complex and varied calls of birds are a testament to the richness of natural auditory communication.

Chemical signals, or pheromones, are another fascinating form of animal communication. These chemical substances are released into the environment and detected by other animals, triggering specific behaviors. Ants, for instance, use so-called pheromones to communicate and organize their colonies. When an ant finds food, it can guide other ants to the food source by leaving a pheromone trail back to the nest. This efficient communication system allows ants to work together in a highly organized manner.

Similarly, many mammals use pheromones to mark territories, signal reproductive status, or identify group members. Certain types of fish, like minnows, release alarm chemicals into the water when they're injured. This chemical signal warns other fish nearby to swim away and hide from danger. Another example is from moths, where females release particular pheromones into the air to attract males from miles away. These chemical signals guide the males directly to the females, even in the dark or over long distances. This shows just how powerful chemical communication can be in the animal world!

Tactile signals involve touch and vibrations, often used in close-range communication. Bees, for example, perform the "waggle dance" to indicate the direction and distance of a food source to other hive members. The bee waggles its body and moves in a figure-eight pattern, with the angle of the dance indicating the direction relative to the Sun. This tactile communication is crucial for the hive's survival, ensuring bees can efficiently gather food. Another example concerns elephants, which use low-frequency vibrations transmitted through the ground to communicate over long distances. These vibrations can convey information about threats, social interactions, or mating opportunities. Sea otters hold hands while they sleep to stay together in the water. This adorable behavior helps them stay close to one another, preventing them from drifting apart in the ocean currents.

The purpose of communication in the animal kingdom is multifaceted. Mating and reproduction are primary drivers, as animals need to attract mates and ensure the continuation of their species. Visual displays, vocal calls, and chemical signals all play a role in this process. Social organization is another critical aspect, as animals need to maintain group structures, establish hierarchies, and coordinate activities. For instance, wolves use a combination of vocalizations, body language, and scents to establish pack dynamics and coordinate hunts. Predation and defense are also critical reasons for communication. Animals must warn each other of danger, coordinate attacks, or deter predators. For example, a meerkat's alarm call alerts the group to the presence of a predator, allowing them to take evasive action.

Communication in the animal kingdom is as diverse and complex as the creatures themselves. From the bright feathers of a peacock to the silent pheromone trails of ants, these signals are vital for survival and social interaction. Plenty of fascinating examples highlight the sophisticated communication systems that animals have developed to thrive in their environments. Understanding these communication methods gives us a deeper appreciation of the natural world and the intricate ways animals interact with each other.

THE MYSTERIES OF BIOLUMINESCENT CREATURES

Imagine walking through a forest at night and seeing tiny lights flickering all around you. This enchanting display is not from fairy lights but fireflies, which use bioluminescence to **communicate and attract** mates. Bioluminescence is the production of light by living organisms through a chemical reaction involving two key components: luciferin and luciferase. When luciferin reacts with oxygen in the presence of luciferase, it produces light. This reaction is incredibly efficient, releasing energy in the form of light with very little heat, making these organisms glow in the dark.

Fireflies are perhaps the most well-known bioluminescent creatures. These small beetles produce light in their abdomens to attract mates. Each firefly species has its unique pattern of flashes, helping them identify potential partners. The light show you see on a summer night is a complex communication system. Male fireflies fly around, flashing their lights, while females respond with their own signals, creating a captivating dance of lights.

But the world of bioluminescence extends far beyond fireflies. In the deep sea, where sunlight never reaches, creatures like the anglerfish use bioluminescence to lure prey. The anglerfish has a bioluminescent lure that dangles in front of its mouth, attracting unsuspecting prey in the darkness. When a curious fish gets too close, the anglerfish snaps it up in a swift motion. This adaptation is crucial for survival in the ocean's pitch-black depths, where food can be scarce.

Glowworms in caves and forests use bioluminescence to attract insects to their sticky silk threads. The light produced by glowworms is incredibly bright and serves as a beacon in the darkness. The ceiling can appear like a starry night sky in caves, with thousands of glowworms creating a mesmerizing display. This light helps the glowworms catch more prey, ensuring their survival.

Jellyfish, like the Aequorea victoria, are another group of bioluminescent creatures. These jellyfish produce a beautiful blue-green light along their edges, creating an ethereal glow in the water. The light is produced by specialized cells called photocytes, which contain the chemicals needed for bioluminescence. Bioluminescence can serve multiple purposes for jellyfish, including attracting mates, deterring predators, and communicating with other jellyfish.

Bioluminescence serves various functions in the animal kingdom. One of the primary uses is attracting mates. In many species, the ability to produce light is a signal of fitness, helping individuals find and attract partners. Fireflies are a prime example, but other bioluminescent creatures also use light to enhance their chances of reproduction.

Another significant function of bioluminescence is **luring prey**. Deep-sea creatures like the anglerfish use bioluminescent lures to attract potential prey in the darkness. This strategy is highly effective, allowing them to catch food in an environment where visibility is limited. Similarly, glowworms use light to attract insects to their traps, ensuring a steady food supply.

Bioluminescence also plays a role in **defense mechanisms**. Some animals use light to startle predators, creating a sudden flash that can confuse or deter an attacker. Others use counter-illumination, producing light on their undersides to match the light from the surface, effectively camouflaging themselves from predators below. This adaptation is common in deep-sea fish and squid, helping them avoid detection in the dimly lit ocean depths.

You don't have to travel to the deep sea to observe bioluminescence. Seasonal firefly displays can be seen in many parts of the world during warm summer nights. Watching fireflies light up a field is a magical experience, connecting you to the wonders of nature. If you ever have the chance, visit a bioluminescent bay, such as Mosquito Bay in Puerto Rico. These unique places are home to bioluminescent plankton that light up when disturbed, creating a glowing trail in the water. The sight of glowing water moving with the waves is spectacular.

HOW PLANTS "EAT" SUNLIGHT: PHOTOSYNTHESIS EXPLAINED

Photosynthesis allows plants to use sunlight and water to produce the food they need to grow. In turn, plants become the foundation of the food chain, providing energy for all animal life while also producing the oxygen we breathe. Think about it! Photosynthesis is crucial for all life on Earth! That's why knowing how it works in basic terms is a way to appreciate yet another wonder in nature.

Going through the process may sound complicated, but we will get there.

The process is made possible by **chlorophyll**, the green pigment found in plant leaves. Chlorophyll captures sunlight and initiates a series of reactions that transform light energy into chemical energy.

Photosynthesis has **two main stages**: light-dependent reactions and light-independent reactions. Let's break it down!

In the **first stage**, the **light-dependent reactions**, sunlight is absorbed by the chlorophyll in the thylakoid membranes inside the chloroplasts of plant leaves. This sunlight energy helps split water molecules into **oxygen, protons, and electrons.** We will talk about the two fellows, "protons" and "electrons," in the chemistry section; for now, it is just essential to understand that these are tiny particles that form part of the atoms, which are, in turn, building blocks of matter. However, the oxygen is released into the air, which is actually the oxygen we breathe. At the same time, the protons and electrons are used to create energy-rich molecules called **ATP** and **NADPH**. We will call these important guys "Eddy" and "Ned." These molecules act like little energy packets the plant will use in the next stage.

The **light-independent reactions**, or the **Calvin Cycle**, form the **second stage** and occur in a different part of the chloroplasts called the stroma. This stage doesn't need sunlight, so it's sometimes called the "dark reaction." In the Calvin Cycle, Eddy and Ned, from the first stage, help turn carbon dioxide from the air into glucose, a type of sugar that plants use for energy and growth, the same way we do and will find out about later in the chapter on the human body.

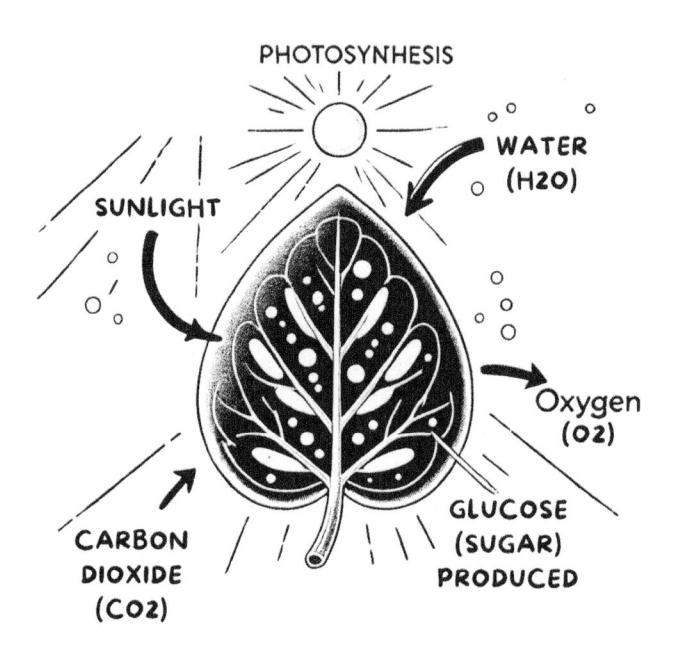

PHOTOSYNHESIS

SUNLIGHT

WATER (H2O)

CARBON DIOXIDE (CO2)

Oxygen (O2)

GLUCOSE (SUGAR) PRODUCED

In summary, sunlight helps break water molecules and create energy in the first stage—Eddy and Ned. Then, in the second stage, that energy turns carbon dioxide into glucose, which fuels the plant's growth.

Photosynthesis is not just a fascinating process; it's crucial for life on Earth. Plants produce oxygen as a byproduct of photosynthesis, which is essential for humans and animals to breathe. Without plants, our atmosphere would lack the oxygen needed to sustain life, as most living organisms consume oxygen and produce carbon dioxide instead. Additionally, photosynthesis forms the foundation of the food chain. Plants are primary producers, meaning they create their own food and serve as a food source for herbivores, which in turn are eaten by carnivores. In the grand story of nature, **herbivores** are the plant-loving munchers who happily nibble on leaves and veggies. At the same time, **carnivores** are daring hunters who chase after other animals, each playing their unique role in keeping the world balanced and exciting. This chain of energy flow starts with the simple act of plants converting sunlight into glucose.

You can see the importance of photosynthesis in everyday life. For instance, when you eat a salad, you're consuming the energy plants have stored through photosynthesis. When you breathe in, you're inhaling oxygen produced by plants. Even the wooden furniture in your home is made from trees that grew by converting sunlight into energy and producing oxygen during their lifetime.

To experience photosynthesis firsthand, you may try a simple experiment called leaf chromatography. This activity allows you to separate the different pigments in leaves, revealing the hidden colors contributing to photosynthesis. You'll need a few leaves, rubbing alcohol, coffee filters, and a jar. Crush the leaves and place them in the jar with rubbing alcohol. Let them sit for a few hours to extract the pigments. Then, place a strip of coffee filter paper in the jar, allowing it to absorb the liquid. Different colors appear as the liquid travels up the paper, representing the various pigments involved in photosynthesis. There are plenty of videos on the internet to check out further details.

Another engaging experiment is observing oxygen bubbles in aquatic plants. Submerge a piece of an aquatic plant like Elodea in a water-filled container and place it in sunlight. Or pay attention to such plants next time you see a fish aquarium. You'll notice tiny bubbles forming on the leaves, which are oxygen bubbles produced during photosynthesis. This simple observation visually demonstrates how plants produce oxygen, making the process of photosynthesis tangible and exciting.

Photosynthesis is a marvel of nature. It transforms sunlight into the energy that fuels life on Earth. The impact of this process is profound and far-reaching, from the food we eat to the air we breathe.

THE AMAZING WORLD OF MICROORGANISMS

Microorganisms might be tiny, but they play massive roles in our world. These microscopic life forms come in many shapes and sizes, including bacteria, viruses, fungi, and protists.

Bacteria are single-celled organisms that can live almost anywhere: in soil, water, and even in your yogurt. They can be beneficial, like those that help digest food, or harmful, like those that cause infections.

Viruses, on the other hand, are not considered fully alive. They are infectious agents that hijack the machinery of living cells to reproduce, causing diseases like the flu and the common cold.

Fungi are decomposers, breaking down dead matter to recycle nutrients back into the ecosystem. You'll find fungi in many places, from the mold on old bread to the mushrooms in your backyard.

BACTERIA   **VIRUS**   **FUNGI**

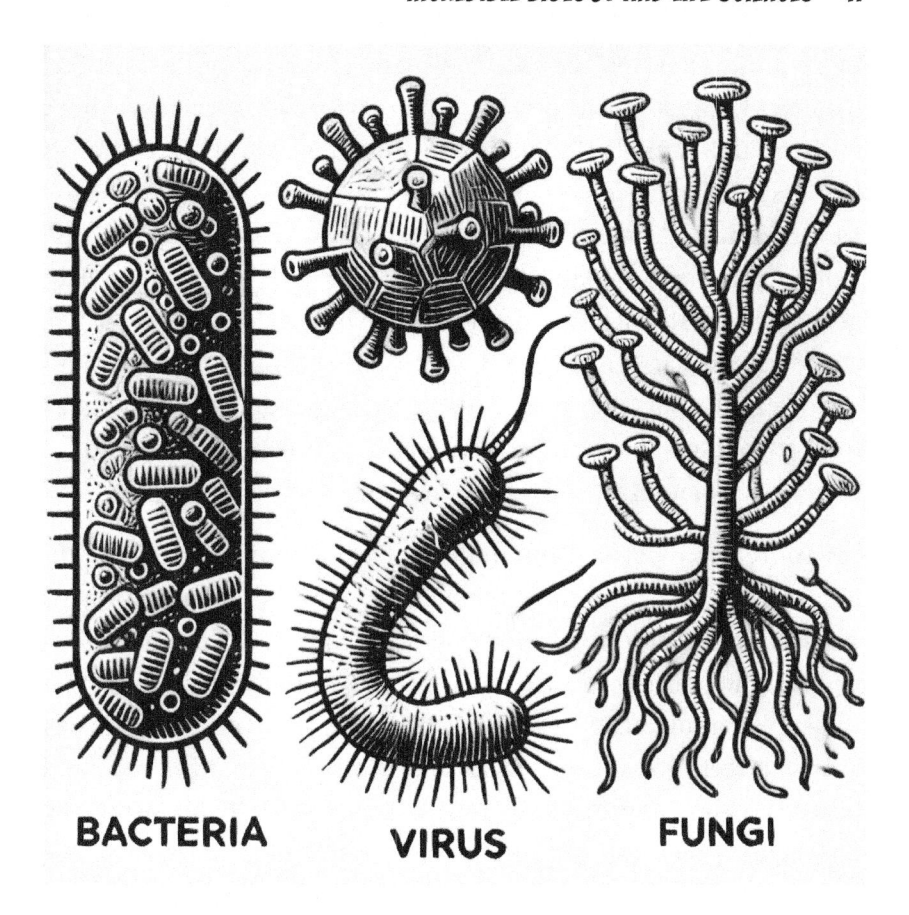

Protists are a diverse group of simple organisms that don't fit neatly into the other categories. They can be plant like, such as algae that produce oxygen through photosynthesis, or animal-like, such as amoebas that move and eat other microorganisms.

In ecosystems, microorganisms are the unsung heroes. They perform crucial tasks that keep the environment healthy and balanced. One of their key roles is **decomposition**. When plants and animals die, fungi and bacteria break down their remains, turning them into simpler substances that enrich the soil. This process recycles nutrients, making them available for new plants to grow. **Nitrogen fixation** is another critical function performed by certain bacteria in the soil. Not many are aware of this. Critical means, in this case, absolutely essential for the survival of both humans and animals on Earth. This so-called nitrogen fixation is like a secret handshake between tiny bacteria and plants. These clever bacteria take nitrogen from the air, which plants can't use alone, and transform it into a unique form that plants need to grow big and strong. This magical teamwork helps our crops, like corn and wheat, grow healthy and full of nutrients. Without nitrogen fixation, our plants would struggle, and so would our food supply, making this process one of nature's most vital tricks to keep our plates full and our bodies nourished.

Microorganisms also profoundly impact human health. Our gut microbiome, a community of trillions of bacteria living in our intestines, is vital for digestion and overall health. These beneficial bacteria help break down food, produce vitamins, and protect against harmful pathogens. On the flip side, some microorganisms are pathogens that cause diseases. Viruses, like influenza, and bacteria, like Streptococcus, can make us sick, highlighting the dual nature of these tiny organisms. Understanding the balance between beneficial and harmful microorganisms is key to maintaining health.

Bacteria also affect whether or not our eatables remain edible, particularly during **food storage**. Hence, it is essential to understand why and under which conditions food degradation typically happens. First, temperature plays a huge role. Bacteria love warm environments, especially between 4°C and 60°C (40°F and 140°F)—this is known as the "danger zone." In this range, bacteria can multiply quickly, turning fresh food into something you wouldn't want to eat in no time. That's why we refrigerate food, keeping it below about 4°C (40°F), slowing down bacterial growth. Next, many bacteria thrive in the presence of oxygen. Foods left exposed to air can become a playground for bacteria that need oxygen to survive. However, some types of bacteria can even grow without oxygen, so sealed, vacuum-packed, or canned foods can spoil if not handled correctly. Moisture is another critical factor. Bacteria love damp environments and need water to thrive, so foods with high water content, like fresh fruits, meats, and dairy products, spoil faster than dry foods like rice or flour.

So, to keep bacteria at bay, it's all about controlling temperature, limiting oxygen exposure, and reducing moisture. Otherwise, your food might turn into a bacteria buffet! You might wonder how a jar of honey found in an ancient Egyptian tomb, over 3,000 years old, could still be edible. It sounds like magic, but it's actually science at work! Honey is naturally equipped with properties that make it almost impossible for bacteria to grow. So was the condition of how it was stored. As we discussed earlier, moisture is one of the critical factors for bacteria to thrive, and honey has a very low moisture content. It is so dense and sticky that there's hardly any free water for bacteria to use. Without that moisture, bacteria can't multiply easily and spoil the honey. Besides the humidity, the low acidity of honey creates an environment that's too harsh for most bacteria and microorganisms to survive. Acidity is expressed as a pH value, which we will discuss later in the chemistry chapter.

For a fun and educational activity, observe yeast at work in baking. Yeast, a type of fungus, is responsible for making bread rise. Yeast mixed with sugar and warm water begins to ferment, producing carbon dioxide gas. This gas gets trapped in the dough, causing it to expand and rise. Next time you're baking bread or visiting a bakery, take a moment to watch the dough rising. Reflect on the power of these tiny organisms and how they transform simple ingredients into delicious bread.

Another intriguing activity is observing mold growth in food. Mold is a fungus that grows on organic matter, and it's fascinating (and a bit gross) to watch how quickly it can spread. Choose foods like bread, fruit, or cheese that spoil quickly. Place them in a safe spot and observe daily changes. You'll see fuzzy patches of mold appearing and spreading. This process is a visible example of decomposition in action. Reflect on how mold breaks down food and returns nutrients to the environment. You might also consider the chemical reactions involved, connecting this observation to later discussions on chemistry in this book.

Microorganisms are everywhere, performing vital functions that sustain life on Earth. Whether they help plants grow, aid in digestion, or break down dead matter, these tiny life forms are essential to our world. Understanding their roles and observing their activities can deepen your appreciation for the incredible complexity of life, even at the microscopic level.

DNA: THE BLUEPRINT OF LIFE

Let's take a journey into the blueprint of life—DNA! Imagine a cookbook filled with every recipe for life itself, from the color of your eyes to your ability to taste certain flavors. This cookbook is called DNA, or deoxyribonucleic acid, and it's the instruction manual for everything that makes you, well, you. DNA is microscopically tiny and can be found in each and every one of our cells. It is shaped like a twisted ladder or double helix. The sides of the ladder are made from sugar and phosphate, while the rungs are pairs of so-called nitrogenous bases: **adenine (A)** always pairs with **thymine (T)**, and **cytosine (C)** pairs with **guanine (G)**. These base pairs form the genetic code that determines all your traits.

A C T G

DNA double helix

Genes are like individual recipes in this DNA cookbook. Each gene carries the instructions for making proteins, which are the building blocks of our bodies. For example, the gene for eye color will decide what pigment fills your iris. Different combinations of genes make each person unique, and your DNA is a mix of both of your parents. That's why you might have your mom's eyes but your dad's hair!

DNA also has a super important job—replication. Before a cell divides, it copies its DNA to ensure each new cell gets the same set of instructions. This starts with an enzyme called helicase, which unwinds the DNA ladder. Then, DNA polymerase adds new base pairs—A with T, and C with G—forming two identical double helixes. This process is how we grow, repair our bodies, and stay alive!

Now, let's talk about how traits are passed down. Traits are determined by **dominant and recessive genes**. Dominant genes appear like the bossy older sibling—even if you have only one copy. Recessive genes are more shy and only appear if you have two copies. For instance, brown eyes are dominant, and blue eyes are recessive. If you inherit one gene for brown eyes and one for blue, your eyes will be brown since the brown-eye gene is in charge.

Not all changes in DNA are bad—some are actually helpful! These changes, called mutations, create variation in a species and can help animals adapt to their environment. For example, a mutation might give a butterfly wings that blend into the forest better, helping it avoid predators. While some mutations cause diseases, they're also a crucial part of evolution and the diversity of life on Earth.

Want to see DNA up close? You can do a simple experiment with strawberries! By mashing strawberries with soap, salt, and water, then adding rubbing alcohol, you'll see the DNA float to the top like white, stringy blobs. It's a cool way to see the invisible instructions that guide life.

Here are some fun facts: Humans share about 60% of their DNA with bananas! The axolotl, a type of salamander, has a genome ten times larger than ours, allowing it to regenerate lost limbs. These facts show how amazing and diverse DNA is across all living things.

DNA is the code that makes life possible. It tells our bodies how to grow, heal, and pass on traits to the next generation. DNA connects every living thing on Earth through its complex structure and processes in one big, beautiful web of life.

We are concluding our journey into biology and life, connecting the microscopic world to the grand diversity of life on Earth. Understanding these concepts enriches our appreciation of nature and lays the foundation for exploring the human body and the physical and chemical principles that govern our universe; before doing so, and as we are talking about the universe, let's dive into space…

CHAPTER THREE
WONDERS OF ASTRONOMY AND SPACE SCIENCE

From the tiny world of microorganisms, we make a giant leap into space, another science field with many wonders. The exciting world of **Astronomy and Space Science**, where we explore the vast playground of the universe! Space is full of wonders that capture our imagination and help scientists unlock the secrets of how everything works—from the smallest atoms to the biggest stars. In this chapter, we'll dive into our cosmic neighborhood, the **Solar System**, and learn about Earth's constant companion, the **Moon**. We'll also venture beyond our solar system to discover distant **Planets** and unravel the mysteries of **Stars** and **Black Holes**. The fascinating concepts we explore here will help us understand key principles and needs of chemistry, physics, and Earth sciences, which we'll dive into later in the book. Get ready to journey through the **Milky Way** and beyond, where the wonders of space await!

THE SOLAR SYSTEM: OUR COSMIC NEIGHBORHOOD

Our solar system is a magnificent collection of celestial bodies, all bound together by the Sun's gravitational pull, our central star. The **Sun**, a massive ball of hydrogen and helium, provides the light and heat necessary for life on Earth. Also, picture the Sun as a grand conductor in the center of a cosmic orchestra, with each planet as a musician following its lead. The planets dance gracefully around the Sun in perfect harmony, each on its own unique path or **orbit**. Like a merry-go-round, they spin in circles, pulled by the Sun's gentle but powerful gravity, ensuring they never stray too far from their bright, warm leader. Its intense gravitational field keeps everything else in the solar system, from the smallest asteroid to the largest gas giant in orbit—or influences its path. The planets, our closest neighbors in space, are divided into two main categories: terrestrial planets and gas giants.

Hence, let's take a tour starting with the fascinating family known as the **terrestrial planets**: Mercury, Venus, Earth, and Mars. These four rocky siblings each have unique personalities and stories to tell.

First, we visit **Mercury**, the smallest and swiftest, racing around the Sun like a speedster on a hot track. But beware! Mercury's extreme days and nights are a wild roller coaster of temperatures. Without a thick atmosphere to keep things cozy, its days are blazing hot, and its nights are freezing cold, like an endless game of "hot and cold"—only very real!

Next is **Venus**, Earth's "sister planet," though she's quite different in personality. Venus is like a pressure cooker on overdrive, wrapped in a thick blanket of sulfuric acid clouds. Her atmosphere is so dense and heavy that it would squish you flat in seconds! And if you think Mercury is hot, think again—Venus has him beat, holding the title of the hottest planet in the solar system, thanks to her super-efficient heat-trapping atmosphere. Here's something fascinating about her. A Venus day actually lasts longer than a year! While Venus takes about 225 Earth days to complete one orbit around the Sun, it takes a staggering 243 Earth days to complete one rotation on its axis.

Then, we arrive at **Earth**, our beloved home and the third rock from the Sun. Earth is the perfect party host, providing everything we need—liquid water, a comfy atmosphere, and just the correct temperatures—to support an incredible variety of life forms, including us! No wonder Earth is the only planet we know of buzzing with life.

Finally, we head to **Mars**, the red planet with a thin, chilly atmosphere mostly made of carbon dioxide. Mars is like the rugged adventurer of the group, with its rusty red surface covered in iron oxide, giving it that signature Martian hue. This planet boasts some record-breaking landmarks, too! Imagine a volcano so massive it would dwarf any on Earth—Olympus Mons—and a vast canyon that makes the Grand Canyon look like a small crack —Valles Marineris. Mars may be cold, but it's full of wonders waiting to be explored!

Together, these four rocky planets comprise a remarkable and diverse ensemble, each contributing its own chapter to the epic story of our solar system. From blistering heat to frigid cold, from nurturing life to inspiring exploration, the terrestrial planets invite us to explore, learn, and appreciate the incredible diversity of worlds that share our Sun's warm embrace.

Beyond the rocky realms of the terrestrial planets, we enter the grand domain of the **gas giants**—Jupiter, Saturn, Uranus, and Neptune. First up is **Jupiter**, the colossal king of the solar system. Imagine a planet so enormous that you could fit 11 Earths side by side across its diameter! Jupiter is not just giant; it's also home to the famous **Great Red Spot**, a gigantic storm swirling like a cosmic whirlpool for over 400 years—a tempest that's truly stood the test of time.

Next, we glide over to **Saturn**, the second-largest planet that never fails to dazzle with its magnificent rings. Saturn's rings are like a glittering necklace, made of countless particles of ice and rock, some as small as grains of sand, others as large as boulders. They circle the planet in a breathtaking display that makes Saturn the jewel of our solar system.

Then there's **Uranus**, the quirky giant with a unique twist—literally! Uranus spins on its side, making it look like it's rolling around the Sun in a playful sideways tumble. Its cool blue-green hue comes from methane clouds in its atmosphere, giving it a tranquil, otherworldly appearance.

Finally, we reach **Neptune**, the farthest of the gas giants, a planet known for its wild and windy personality. Neptune's atmosphere whips up some of the fastest winds in the solar system. Like Jupiter, it has its own dark spots—massive storms that rage across its surface, adding a touch of mystery to this distant, icy world.

Our solar system is full of wonders beyond the main planets! It also includes dwarf planets and moons. **Dwarf planets**, like Pluto, Ceres, and Eris, may be smaller than the main planets, but they still travel around the Sun. Interestingly, Pluto was, for a time, considered the ninth planet before being reclassified as a dwarf planet in 2006. **Moons**, or natural satellites, orbit the planets, and some, like Jupiter's Ganymede and Saturn's Titan, are even larger than Mercury! These fascinating celestial bodies, each with their own unique features and environments, make our cosmic neighborhood even more impressive.

Asteroids and **comets**, often considered the leftovers of planetary formation, play crucial roles in the solar system. The Asteroid Belt, located between Mars and Jupiter, is home to countless rocky bodies ranging in size from tiny pebbles to massive objects like Ceres, the giant asteroid. Asteroids can provide valuable information about the early solar system and the processes that led to planet formation. Comets, composed of ice, dust, and rocky material, originate from the far reaches of the solar system in regions like the Kuiper Belt and the Oort Cloud. When a comet approaches the Sun, its ice vaporizes, creating a glowing coma and a spectacular tail stretching millions of kilometers. Famous comets, like Halley's Comet, which appears every 76 years, have fascinated humanity for centuries and inspired countless myths and legends. Suppose you're lucky enough to catch a glimpse of a comet. In that case, you'll see it blazing brilliantly, its nucleus glowing at the center like a bright gem, while its tail fans out like a glowing ribbon, pointing away from the Sun. The next opportunity to see Halley's Comet will be in the year 2061, by the way…

Exploring the solar system has been a monumental endeavor, with numerous missions advancing our understanding of these distant worlds. The Voyager probes, launched in 1977, have provided invaluable insights into the outer planets. Voyager 1 and 2 conducted flybys of Jupiter, Saturn, Uranus, and Neptune, sending back stunning images and data that revolutionized our knowledge of these gas giants. Voyager 1 is now the farthest human-made object from Earth, traveling through interstellar space.

Mars has been a primary focus of exploration, with missions like the Curiosity and Perseverance rovers uncovering the planet's secrets. Curiosity, which landed in 2012, has been exploring the Gale Crater, analyzing rock samples, and searching for signs of past microbial life.

Its successor, Perseverance, landed in 2021 in the Jezero Crater. It has advanced instruments to study its geology and search for signs of ancient life. These missions aim to pave the way for future human exploration of Mars.

The New Horizons mission to Pluto was another groundbreaking achievement. Launched in 2006, New Horizons conducted a flyby of Pluto in 2015, providing the first close-up images of this distant world. The mission revealed Pluto's complex terrain, including icy mountains and vast plains, and discovered that the dwarf planet has a thin atmosphere and active geological processes.

The exploration of our solar system continues to push the boundaries of human knowledge and imagination. Each mission brings new discoveries, revealing the wonders of our cosmic neighborhood and inspiring future generations to reach for the stars. The vastness of space, with its myriad celestial bodies, offers endless opportunities for exploration and discovery, reminding us of our place in the universe and the boundless potential of human curiosity and ingenuity.

THE MOON: EARTH'S CELESTIAL COMPANION

Imagine gazing up at the night sky and spotting the Moon glowing softly and lighting up the darkness. This celestial companion has captivated human imagination for thousands of years. But have you ever wondered how the Moon came to be? According to the giant impact hypothesis, a colossal collision occurred around 4.5 billion years ago between the early Earth and a Mars-sized body. The impact was so powerful that it sent a massive amount of debris flying into orbit around Earth. Over time, this scattered debris slowly came together, eventually forming the Moon we know today.

The Moon's surface is a mix of maria, highlands, and craters. The "maria," Latin for oceans, are vast, dark plains formed by ancient volcanic eruptions. The name originates from ancient interpretations that the Moon's surface was covered by oceans. As we touched on Latin, the word "lunar," often used on topics related to the Moon, comes from the Latin word *luna*, meaning "moon." Back to its surface: The highlands are older, lighter areas covered with craters. In contrast, the craters result from asteroid impacts over billions of years.

Every month, the Moon puts on a magical show just for us, changing its shape as it moves through a series of **phases**. This monthly performance comes from the ever-changing positions of the Earth, Moon, and Sun. When the Moon sneaks between the Earth and the Sun, it hides in shadow, giving us the mysterious **New Moon**. As the Moon continues its orbit around Earth, we see more of its bright side, unveiling the delicate **Waxing Crescent**, the half-lit **First Quarter**, and then the almost complete **Waxing Gibbous**.

Then comes the grand finale—the **Full Moon**, when the Moon is fully lit up, shining bright on the opposite side of Earth from the Sun. But just when you think the show is over, it reverses again. The light begins to fade through the **Waning Gibbous**, the half-lit **Last Quarter**, and the silver-thin **Waning Crescent** phases until, like a magician's trick, we're back to the **New Moon**.

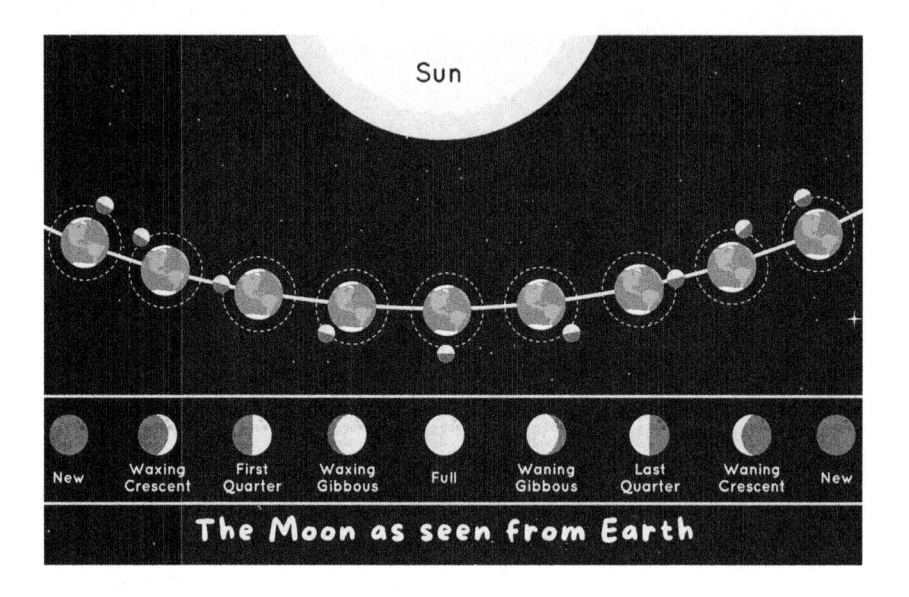

The Moon as seen from Earth

This enchanting dance of shadows and light reminds us of the Moon's constant yet ever-changing presence in our night sky—a celestial performance we're lucky to enjoy every month.

This fascinating "moon cycle" takes about 29.5 days to complete and has been a natural timekeeper for humans across generations. Long before modern calendars, people looked to the changing Moon as a reliable way to measure more extended periods beyond the day. This lunar cycle became the foundation for the months we use today, offering a beautifully simple and tangible way to track the passage of time. So, every time you glance up at the Moon, remember that it's not just lighting up the night—it's also marking the rhythm of our lives, just as it has for countless generations.

But the Moon is not just a shiny timekeeper in space; it also profoundly shapes the rhythms of life on Earth.

The Moon's gravitational pull—think of it as the Moon's "weight" in space—has a powerful impact on Earth's **tides**, causing the rhythmic rise and fall of ocean waters along our coastlines. This invisible force drives the regular movement of the tides we observe each day. Tides are the result of the Moon's gravity pulling on Earth's oceans, creating bulges in the water.

As these bulges move around the planet, they cause the familiar high and low tides. During full and new moons, when the Sun, Moon, and Earth align, this gravitational pull is the strongest, leading to **spring tides**—times when high tides are higher and low tides are lower. On the other hand, when the Sun and Moon form a right angle with Earth, their gravitational forces partially cancel each other out, resulting in **neap tides**, where the difference between high and low tides is less extreme.

This ongoing dance between the Earth, Moon, and Sun not only shapes our oceans but also plays a crucial role in marine life's behavior and the health of coastal ecosystems, making it an essential part of life on our planet.

This "dance of the three" also has visual culminations every now and then: You may have heard about **eclipses**.

Those spectacular events occur when the Earth, Moon, and Sun align in specific ways. A **solar eclipse** happens when the Moon passes between the Earth and the Sun, casting a shadow on Earth and temporarily blocking the Sun's light. The area where the Sun is wholly blocked is called the **umbra**; where the Sun is partially obscured, it is labeled the **penumbra**. Accordingly, there are three solar eclipse types: **total**, **partial**, and **annular**. During a total solar eclipse, the Moon completely covers the Sun, revealing the Sun's outer atmosphere, the corona. Observing a solar eclipse requires safety precautions, such as using special glasses or pinhole projectors to protect your eyes from the Sun's harmful rays.

A **lunar eclipse** occurs when the Earth comes between the Sun and the Moon, casting a shadow on the Moon. This can happen only during a full moon. During a total lunar eclipse, the Earth's shadow gives the Moon a reddish hue, often called a "Blood Moon."

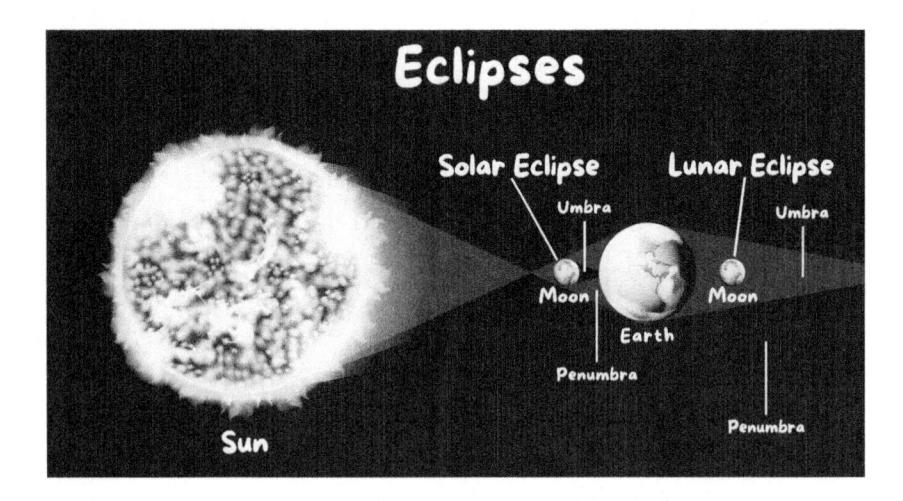

Exploring the Moon has been a monumental achievement in human history. The Apollo missions, conducted by NASA from 1961 to 1972, were a series of manned missions that culminated in the first Moon landing in 1969. Apollo 11 saw astronauts Neil Armstrong and Buzz Aldrin walk on the lunar surface, leaving footprints that will remain for a long time. These missions provided invaluable scientific data, collected moon rocks, and advanced our understanding of the Moon's composition and history.

There are plans to return humans to the Moon and establish a sustainable presence. The program may also pave the way for future lunar bases, where astronauts can live and work for extended periods. This will serve as a testing ground for technologies and strategies for future missions to Mars and beyond. The Moon, our celestial companion, continues to be a source of inspiration, scientific discovery, and exploration.

PLANETS BEYOND OUR SOLAR SYSTEM

Imagine gazing up at the night sky and wondering if there are other worlds out there, circling stars just like our Earth circles the Sun. Well, you're not alone in that curiosity! These distant worlds, known as exoplanets, exist far beyond our solar system, and they come in all sorts of shapes and sizes—from rocky planets like Earth to massive gas giants that dwarf even Jupiter. Finding these exoplanets is challenging, but astronomers have developed clever techniques to track them down.

One of the most exciting finds is **Kepler-186f**, an Earth-sized exoplanet in its star's "habitable zone"—the sweet spot where conditions might be just right for liquid water. Kepler-186f orbits a red dwarf star about 500 light-years away, and its size and location make it a prime candidate in the search for life. Another thrilling discovery is **Proxima Centauri b**, the closest known exoplanet to Earth. It circles around Proxima Centauri, a red dwarf star just over four light-years away, and like Kepler-186f, it's also in the habitable zone, sparking the imagination with the possibility of life.

The potential for life on these exoplanets hinges on a few key factors. The most crucial is whether the planet resides in the **habitable zone**, where temperatures are just right for liquid water, a key ingredient for life as we know it. The atmosphere is also a big deal—a stable atmosphere can regulate temperature and protect the planet from harmful radiation. The presence of gases like oxygen and methane might hint at biological activity. And, of course, the planet's size and composition matter, too. Rocky planets with solid surfaces are much more likely to support life than those made of gas.

Take Earth, for example. It's the perfect blueprint for a habitable planet. We're snugly situated in the Sun's habitable zone, with the proper temperatures for liquid water. Our atmosphere is a life-friendly mix of gases, including oxygen, nitrogen, and carbon dioxide, and it acts as a protective shield against solar radiation and space debris. Earth's magnetic field adds an extra layer of protection, deflecting harmful solar winds. With liquid water, a stable climate, and diverse ecosystems, Earth is a thriving oasis for life.

Astronomy scientists searching for exoplanets are like cosmic detectives, piecing together clues from the vastness of space. One of the most popular ways they find exoplanets is through the **transit method**. This method involves carefully watching a distant star for tiny dips in brightness. If a planet passes in front of the star from our point of view, it blocks a small portion of the star's light, creating a noticeable "blip" or dip. By monitoring these regular dips, scientists can detect the presence of a planet and even estimate its size based on how much light it blocks.

But that's just one tool in their toolkit! Astronomers also use other methods, like the **radial velocity method**, which measures tiny wobbles in a star's motion caused by an orbiting planet with its gravitational pull. This gives clues about the planet's mass. Another method, **direct imaging**, uses powerful telescopes to capture actual images of exoplanets. However, this is much trickier and rarer due to stars' immense distance and brightness.

Finding exoplanets is a lot like solving a puzzle, and it takes a ton of data to get it right. Scientists must collect and analyze massive amounts of information from telescopes over long periods. And it's not just about spotting planets—once found, they have to figure out what kind of planet it is. Is it a rocky world like Earth or a gas giant like Jupiter? That's where chemistry and Earth sciences come in. By studying the planet's and its sun's movements, masses and sizes can be estimated, which may answer whether the exoplanet is made of rock or gas or has clouds, oceans, or even the potential for life.

This is no small task. It requires deep knowledge of physics to understand the gravitational forces and movements, chemistry to analyze the planet's atmosphere, and Earth sciences to compare these alien worlds to our own. Since all this data comes in numbers, scientists need strong programming skills to write software that can handle complex calculations and massive datasets.

Nowadays, scientists don't just rely on telescopes here on Earth. Some of the most powerful telescopes, like the **Kepler Space Telescope** and **TESS (Transiting Exoplanet Survey Satellite)**, are located in space, orbiting above our planet to get an even clearer view of distant stars without interference from Earth's atmosphere. Together, these earthbound and orbital telescopes provide incredible data, and astronomers are constantly analyzing it, hoping to discover the next exciting exoplanet. The search for exoplanets is a quest to find distant worlds and deepen our understanding of the universe and our place within it!

And here's something to blow your mind: Scientists have discovered more planets than stars in the Milky Way galaxy! This mind-boggling fact is a humbling reminder of the universe's vastness and the endless possibilities for exploration and discovery. Each new exoplanet we find adds another piece to the cosmic puzzle. The quest to find exoplanets continues to inspire our imaginations, pushing the limits of technology and deepening our understanding of the cosmos.

THE LIFE CYCLE OF STARS

You may have had the chance to look up to a cloudless night sky in a dark place with minimal light surrounding you and see countless stars twinkling back at you. Each of those stars is at a different stage in its life cycle, a process that begins in a **nebula**, a giant cloud of gas and dust. These star-forming regions are where new stars are born. Gravity pulls the gas and dust together, and as the material clumps, it starts to heat up, forming a so-called **protostar**, the early stage of star formation. This process can take millions of years, but eventually, within the protostar, something incredible is happening—nuclear fusion. However, what exactly is nuclear fusion?

Think of it like this: Inside a star, tiny particles called hydrogen atoms are packed together under immense pressure and heat. When these hydrogen atoms collide with enough force, they fuse together to form a new atom—helium. This process releases enormous energy, like when you crack a glow stick and it starts to shine, but on a cosmic scale!

This energy is what makes a star shine so brightly. It's the fuel that keeps the star burning for millions, even billions of years. Without **nuclear fusion**, stars wouldn't have the energy to light up the night sky or to keep planets warm and cozy in their orbits. So, in a way, nuclear fusion is like the heart of a star, pumping out the energy that makes life in the universe possible.

A star is now in the main sequence phase of its life, spending most of its life fusing hydrogen into helium in its core. This is a stable period where the outward pressure from nuclear fusion balances the inward pull of gravity. Our Sun is currently in this stage, providing the light and heat that sustain life on Earth. Depending on their mass, stars remain in the main sequence phase for millions to billions of years.

As stars exhaust their hydrogen fuel, they enter the **red giant** phase. The core contracts while the outer layers expand and cool, giving the star a reddish appearance. For medium-sized stars like our Sun, this phase leads to the shedding of outer layers, forming a beautiful planetary nebula. The remaining core becomes a **white dwarf**, a dense, cooling remnant that will eventually fade into a **black dwarf** over billions of years.

Massive stars, on the other hand, take a more dramatic exit. After their **red giant phase**, they undergo further fusion, creating heavier elements until they reach iron. At this point, fusion can no longer sustain the star, and it collapses under its own gravity, resulting in a massive explosion called a **supernova**. The core left behind can become a **neutron star**, an incredibly dense object mostly made of neutrons. If the core is even more massive, it can collapse further into a **black hole**, a point in space with gravity so strong that not even light can escape. We will "dive into" black holes in the next chapter.

As you may have heard, stars have guided explorers and inspired countless myths and legends throughout history. Celestial navigation, the art of using stars for guidance, has been especially crucial for sailors and adventurers. The North Star, Polaris, is famous for its nearly fixed position in the sky, making it a reliable beacon for finding true north. Sailors of the Northern hemisphere would determine their latitude—their distance north of the equator—by measuring the angle of Polaris above the horizon. These techniques were vital for early naval exploration, allowing sailors to navigate vast oceans long before the days of GPS and modern technology.

WONDERS OF ASTRONOMY AND SPACE SCIENCE 69

Did you know that stories associated with constellations have been passed down through generations, weaving stars into human culture? To pick two, we can take the constellation Orion, which, for example, is named after a hunter in Greek mythology. According to the myth, Orion was placed in the sky by Zeus after his death, forever hunting across the heavens. The Pleiades, a cluster of stars in the constellation Taurus, in English, the Bull, is linked to various myths, including the Greek tale of the seven sisters who were transformed into stars to escape the pursuit of said Orion.

The life cycle of stars is a captivating process that spans billions of years, from their birth in nebulas to their final stages as white dwarfs, neutron stars, or black holes. Each stage of a star's life contributes to the richness of the universe, creating new elements and shaping the cosmos. As we gaze at the stars, we are witnessing a continuous cycle of creation and transformation, a testament to the universe's dynamic nature.

THE MYSTERIES OF BLACK HOLES

Imagine an object so dense and powerful that nothing, not even light, can escape as soon as it gets near it. This is a black hole, one of the universe's most enigmatic phenomena. When massive stars collapse under their own gravity, they form black holes at the end of their life cycles. We have already touched on the subject of gravity and will get back to it in a later chapter. For now, think of gravity as its own weight. As the star's core shrinks, its gravity intensifies, creating a region where the escape velocity exceeds the speed of light, which makes it appear black, according to some theories. This boundary region is known as the **event horizon**. Once crossed, any form of matter or radiation is pulled inexorably inward, unable to escape. At the center of a black hole lies a point of infinite density, the **singularity**, where the laws of physics as we know them break down.

Black holes come in various types, each fascinating in its own right. **Stellar black holes** are the remnants of massive stars undergoing supernova explosions. These black holes typically have masses ranging from a few to several tens of times that of our Sun. They are scattered throughout galaxies, often found in binary systems where they can siphon material from companion stars, creating spectacular X-ray emissions. On the other hand, **supermassive black holes** reside at the centers of galaxies, including

WONDERS OF ASTRONOMY AND SPACE SCIENCE 71

our Milky Way. These giants have masses ranging from millions to billions of times that of the Sun. How they grow to such immense sizes remains one of astronomy's great mysteries. **Hypothetical miniature black holes**, if they exist, could form through high-energy cosmic events, like the early moments of the Big Bang. Though never observed, they remain a tantalizing possibility for scientists exploring the universe's origins.

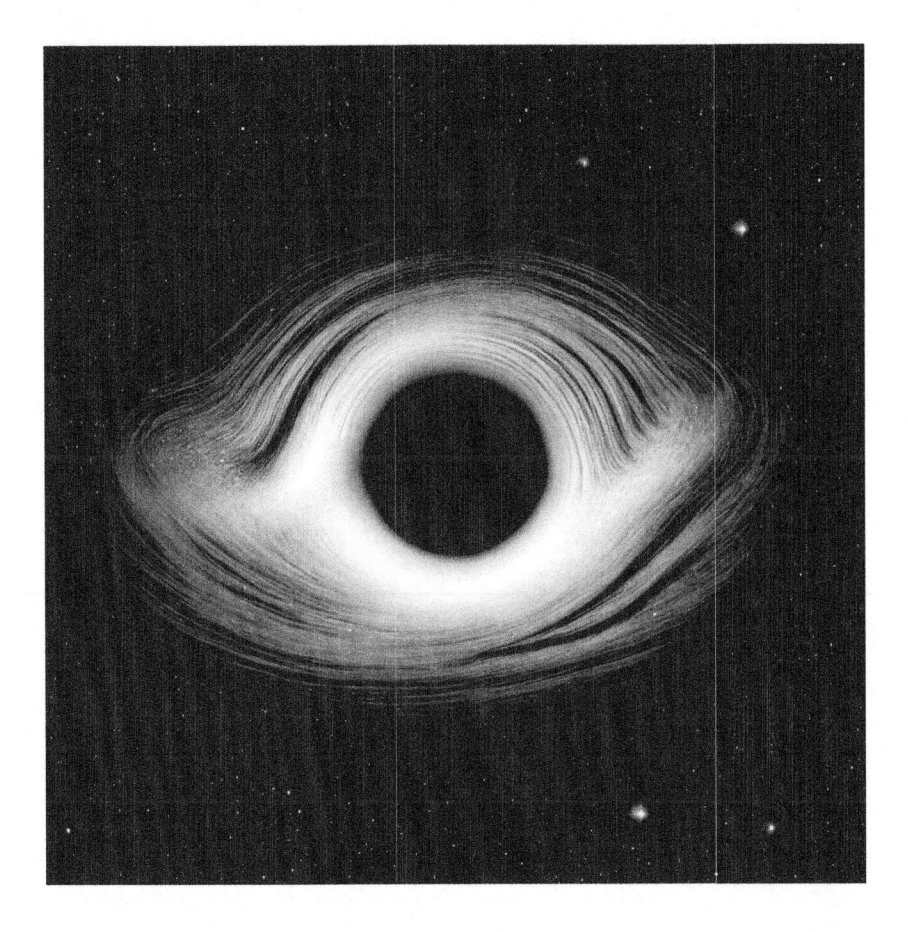

The effects of black holes on their surroundings are nothing short of dramatic. One of the most bizarre phenomena associated with black holes is spaghettification. As an object approaches a black hole, the difference in gravitational pull between its near and far sides becomes extreme. This tidal force stretches the object into a long, thin shape like spaghetti. The closer it gets, the more it's stretched, ultimately torn apart. This process vividly illustrates the immense gravitational forces at play near black holes.

Another feature of black holes is the accretion disk, a swirling mass of gas, dust, and other matter that spirals into the black hole. As material in the accretion disk accelerates inward, it heats up, emitting intense radiation that can be observed across various wavelengths, from X-rays to radio waves. These emissions provide crucial clues for astronomers studying black holes, as the disks are often the only visible evidence of an otherwise invisible object.

To make the concept of black holes more relatable, picture a waterfall. Imagine a river flowing toward the edge of a massive waterfall. The water far from the edge flows calmly, but as it gets closer, it accelerates, pulled by gravity. At the edge, the water plunges down with unstoppable force. The event horizon of a black hole is like the edge of that waterfall. Once you cross it, there's no turning back. The river's calm flow represents the space far from the black hole. At the same time, the accelerating water near the edge symbolizes the intensifying gravitational pull as you approach the event horizon.

Visualizing black holes this way helps demystify these cosmic enigmas, making them more understandable. The universe is filled with wonders that challenge our understanding, and black holes are among the most fascinating. These invisible giants, with their extraordinary gravitational forces and dramatic effects on their surroundings, continue to captivate and inspire, reminding us of the vast and mysterious nature of the cosmos.

EXPLORING THE MILKY WAY GALAXY

Yet again, we are stepping outside on a crisp, clear night. Look up, and there it is—a dense band of stars stretching across the sky like a celestial highway. This breathtaking sight is none other than the Milky Way, our cosmic neighborhood beyond the solar system.

The Milky Way is what scientists call a **spiral galaxy**, which means it has these cool, swirling arms of stars, gas, and dust. These arms aren't just for show—they're star factories, churning out new stars from enormous clouds of gas and dust. The Milky Way's spiral structure isn't just pretty to look at; it's a dynamic dance, with stars being born, living out their lives, and eventually fading away.

Now, if we could zoom into the very heart of the Milky Way, we'd find something truly mind-blowing: the **galactic center**. This is the most bustling, energetic part of our galaxy, home to a supermassive black hole named **Sagittarius A***. This black hole is a heavyweight, packing in the mass of about four million suns! Its gravitational pull is so powerful that it controls the orbits of nearby stars and gas clouds, almost like a cosmic puppet master. The galactic center is a hotspot of activity, with stars whipping around at incredible speeds and bursts of radiation lighting up the region. But here's the catch—this area is shrouded in dense clouds of gas and dust, making it challenging to see directly. Thankfully, scientists have some pretty clever tricks to study this hidden part of our galaxy.

The Milky Way is home to countless fascinating features and objects. The Orion Arm, where our solar system is located, is just one of several spiral arms that wind their way around the galaxy. Each arm contains a mix of young stars, star-forming regions, and remnants of past star formation. In addition to these significant features, the Milky Way contains globular clusters—spherical groups of old stars that orbit the galactic center—and stellar nurseries, where new stars are being born.

Studying the Milky Way requires a variety of tools and methods. Telescopes are the primary instruments, and they come in different types: radio, optical, and infrared. Radio telescopes detect radio waves emitted by celestial objects, allowing us to study regions obscured by dust. Like the Hubble Space Telescope, optical telescopes capture visible light, providing stunning images of stars, nebulae, and galaxies. Infrared telescopes, such as the Spitzer Space Telescope, detect heat radiation, revealing details about cooler objects like star-forming regions and interstellar dust clouds.

Space missions have significantly advanced our understanding of the Milky Way. The Gaia mission, launched by the European Space Agency, aims to create our galaxy's most accurate 3D map. Gaia measures over a billion stars' positions, distances, and motions, providing insights into the Milky Way's structure and evolution. The previously mentioned Hubble Space Telescope, a joint project between NASA and ESA, has captured breathtaking images of the galaxy, revealing its beauty and complexity. These missions and ground-based observations continue to uncover new details about our galactic home.

The Milky Way is vast, containing an estimated 100 to 400 billion stars. To put that into perspective, imagine filling a bucket with grains of sand, with each grain representing a star. You would need millions of buckets to describe all the stars in the Milky Way. This immense number highlights the sheer scale of our galaxy. Another fascinating concept is the galactic year, the time it takes for our solar system to complete one orbit around the galactic center. This journey takes about 225 to 250 million Earth years.

The last time our solar system was in its current position, dinosaurs roamed the Earth.

The Milky Way is not just our home; it's a dynamic and ever-changing environment that offers endless opportunities for exploration and discovery. As we continue to study our galaxy, we acquire a deeper understanding of our place in the universe and the forces that shape our cosmic neighborhood. Each discovery brings us closer to unraveling the mysteries of the Milky Way, inspiring us to look up and wonder about the vast expanse of space that surrounds us.

So, the next time you gaze up at the night sky, remember—you're looking at a tiny slice of a massive, swirling, star-making machine that's constantly changing, just like the universe itself. Cool, right?

Now that we've explored the wonders of our space, let's turn our attention to the intricate workings of the human body. We'll uncover the secrets of human life itself.

CHAPTER FOUR
HUMAN BODY AND HEALTH

Did you know your brain generates enough electricity to power a small light bulb? That's right! This incredible organ, weighing just about one and a half kilograms or three pounds, is the control center of your body, constantly sending signals to keep you alive and functioning. In this chapter, we'll dive deep into the wonders of the human body, starting with the **Human Brain**, where all your thoughts, movements, and senses are managed. We'll explore the **Circulatory System**, the highway that transports blood and oxygen to every part of your body, and look at the **Digestive System**, which turns food into energy. You'll also discover how your **Immune System** is constantly fighting off germs and keeping you healthy, and learn about the **Skeletal System**, which provides the structure and support for all your movements. Finally, we'll uncover the **Science of Sleep**, explaining why it's essential for your body to rest and recharge!

THE HUMAN BRAIN: OUR BODY'S CONTROL CENTER

The human brain is an incredible organ, the command center of our entire body. It is responsible for everything from breathing and heartbeat to thoughts and emotions. It can shape our experiences, memories, and even our sense of self, making it one of the most fascinating and complex structures of known life forms.

As we explore the intricate structure of the human brain, we find it's a complex, finely tuned machine divided into key regions, each with crucial roles to play. The **cerebrum**, the brain's largest part, is where thinking, reasoning, and voluntary actions happen. It's split into two **hemispheres** and divided into **lobes**: the **frontal lobe** handles decision-making and movement, the **parietal lobe** deals with sensory information like touch and pain, the **occipital lobe** handles vision, and the **temporal lobe** deals with memory and speech. Picture the cerebrum as your personal command center, guiding everything from solving math problems to playing the piano.

Just beneath the cerebrum lies the **cerebellum**, a more minor but equally essential part of your brain. It's the control center for balance and coordination. Whether riding a bike, dancing, or simply walking without tripping, your cerebellum ensures your movements are smooth and precise. Think of it as the brain's quality control, ensuring everything you do is executed just right.

You'll find the **brainstem** at the base of the brain, the gatekeeper of essential life functions. It connects your brain to your spinal cord and manages critical activities like heart rhythm, breathing, and digestion. The brainstem comprises three parts: the **midbrain**, **pons**, and **medulla**, each responsible for keeping your body's vital systems running without you even having to think about it.

Cerebrum

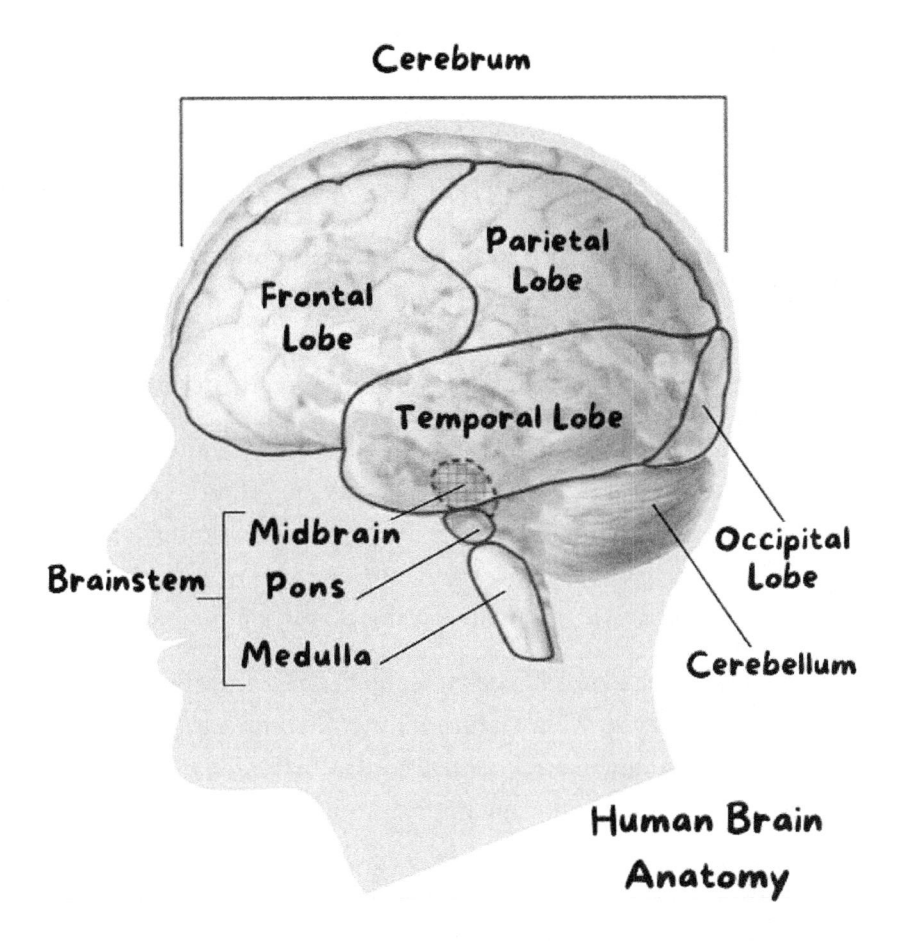

- Frontal Lobe
- Parietal Lobe
- Temporal Lobe
- Occipital Lobe
- Cerebellum

Brainstem
- Midbrain
- Pons
- Medulla

Human Brain Anatomy

As we have explored the different regions of the brain, you might be thinking, "Of course! All these tasks need to be managed somehow." It's a lot to handle, no doubt. So, the next big question is: how does the brain pull it all off?

The brain processes information through a vast network of **neurons**, the brain's communication cells. These little neurons transmit signals, tiny gaps between **synapses**, using chemicals called neurotransmitters. These neurotransmitters carry messages from one neuron to another, enabling everything from muscle contractions to emotional responses. Imagine neurons as the brain's postal service, delivering letters (signals) to various addresses (other neurons) throughout the brain.

Memory is one of the brain's most fascinating functions. It involves storing and recalling information, whether it's the name of your first pet or the capital of France. The **hippocampus**, a seahorse-shaped structure deep within the brain, forms and retrieves memories. Short-term memories are like scribbles on a notepad, easily erased, while long-term memories are more like entries in a diary, lasting for years and sometimes a lifetime.

Sleep cycles are another intriguing aspect of brain function. During sleep, your brain goes through various stages crucial for emotional regulation. It's like the brain's housekeeping service, tidying up the day's experiences and storing them neatly for future use. We will get back to sleep later in this chapter.

Brain plasticity, or neuroplasticity, is the brain's remarkable ability to change and adapt. This feature allows the brain to reorganize itself by forming new neural connections. Whether learning a new language, recovering from an injury, or even picking up a new hobby, your brain constantly adapts. Consider it the brain's version of a personal trainer, continuously working to strengthen and refine its capabilities.

Here are some fun facts about the brain: First, it is about 60% fat, making it the fattiest organ in your body. This fat is crucial for insulating neurons and ensuring efficient signal transmission. Second, as mentioned in the introduction, your brain generates approximately 20 watts of power, enough to power a dim light bulb. Lastly, the brain is not a muscle, even though we often discuss "exercising" it. It contains neurons, blood vessels, and glial cells but no muscle tissue.

THE CIRCULATORY SYSTEM: OUR BODY'S HIGHWAY

To keep everything running smoothly, your body needs two main types of energy carriers: oxygen and nutrients from food. While the digestive system, which we'll explore later, breaks down food and absorbs all the vital nutrients, our fuel, the heart ensures oxygen reaches every corner of your body, enabling efficient fuel use.

Accordingly, the **heart** is the powerful pump at the center of your circulatory system, tirelessly working to keep blood flowing throughout your body. This muscular organ, about the size of your fist, beats approximately 100,000 times a day. It has four chambers: two **atria** on top and two **ventricles** on the bottom. The atria collect blood while the ventricles pump it out. The right side of the heart sends blood to the lungs to pick up oxygen, and the left side pumps this oxygen-rich blood to the rest of the body, where it is needed to function.

Blood vessels are the highways and byways of your circulatory system. **Arteries** carry oxygen-rich blood away to the body's tissues from the heart. They are strong and elastic, built to handle the high pressure from the heart's pumping action. **Veins**, on the other hand, carry oxygen-depleted blood back to the heart. They have valves that prevent blood from flowing backward, ensuring it returns to the heart efficiently. **Capillaries** are the tiny blood vessels that form the bridge between arteries and veins. These are the key locations where oxygen, nutrients, and waste products are exchanged between the blood and the surrounding tissues. These microscopic vessels are so narrow that red blood cells must squeeze through them individually, traveling in a single file.

Blood itself is a fascinating fluid composed of several vital elements. **Red blood cells**, which give blood its color, transport oxygen across the circulatory system. **White blood cells** are the body's defense force, fighting infections and foreign invaders. Later in this chapter, we will get into our defense system, or "Immune System." **Platelets** are cell fragments that play a crucial role in blood clotting, helping to stop bleeding when you get a cut. **Plasma**, the liquid component of blood, is mostly water but contains proteins, hormones, nutrients, and waste products. It makes up about 55% of blood's volume.

The circulatory system works in two main loops: pulmonary and systemic circulations. **Pulmonary circulation** is the path blood takes between the heart and the lungs. It starts when blood leaves the heart's right ventricle and travels to the lungs through the pulmonary arteries. The blood picks up fresh oxygen in the lungs and removes carbon dioxide. Once it's full of oxygen, the blood returns via the pulmonary veins to the heart's left atrium.

Systemic circulation is the journey blood takes between the heart and the rest of the body. The left ventricle pumps this oxygen-rich blood into the aorta, the body's largest artery, from where it travels through a network of arteries, delivering oxygen and nutrients to all the body's tissues. After the oxygen is used up and waste is collected, the now oxygen-depleted blood makes its way back to the heart through the veins, completing the loop and getting ready to start the process all over again.

The circulatory system is vital for transporting oxygen, nutrients, and waste products throughout the body. From these, oxygen delivery is one of its most critical functions. When you inhale, oxygen enters your lungs and binds to hemoglobin molecules in red blood cells. These oxygen-laden cells travel through the bloodstream, delivering oxygen to tissues and organs, enabling them to function properly. Nutrient transport is another essential role. Nutrients from food are absorbed into the bloodstream through the intestinal walls and transported to cells all over your body. Finally, waste removal is crucial for maintaining homeostasis. Metabolic waste products, such as urea and carbon dioxide, are transported by the blood to excretory organs like the lungs and kidneys, where they are expelled from the body.

To understand the circulatory system better, try measuring your heartbeat. Using your fingers, find your pulse on your wrist or neck. Count the beats for 15 seconds and multiply by four to get your heart rate per minute. You can also use a wearable device if you have one. Try measuring your heart rate at rest and then again after doing 10 jumps. Notice how it increases with activity and returns to normal after a few minutes, as the muscles require more oxygen when doing exercises like simple jumps. Average resting heart rates vary by age and sex, but generally, children and teens have higher rates than adults. Regular exercise can improve heart health, making it more efficient at pumping blood.

The circulatory system is an intricate and efficient network that keeps your body functioning smoothly. From the relentless beating of your heart to the microscopic exchange of gases in capillaries, every component plays a vital role in sustaining the body's life.

THE DIGESTIVE SYSTEM: FROM FOOD TO FUEL

In this chapter, we're about to embark on a fascinating journey, following every bite of food as it travels through your body. While I find it exciting and vital for everybody to understand these essentials, I totally get that this might not be everyone's favorite topic. As a parent myself, and remembering discussing these topics with my daughters, I understand. So, if the idea of exploring the journey of food within our bodies doesn't appeal to you, no worries! Feel free to skip ahead to the next chapter.

But let's dive in now: Imagine taking a bite of your favorite sandwich—yum! But what happens next? It all starts in your mouth. When you chew, your teeth break the food into smaller pieces. At the same time, your salivary glands produce **saliva**. Already, the first breakdown of carbohydrates occurs through **enzymes** in the saliva. Enzymes are tiny, specialized helpers in your body that speed up chemical reactions, like breaking down food into nutrients, ensuring everything runs smoothly and efficiently. So, as you chew, your tongue mixes the food with saliva, turning it into a soft, swallowable mass called a bolus. This bolus then travels down the **esophagus**, a muscular tube that connects your mouth to your **stomach**. The esophagus moves the bolus through a series of rhythmic contractions known as peristalsis.

Once the bolus reaches your stomach, it encounters a super-acidic environment. Your stomach lining produces gastric juices containing hydrochloric acid and digestive enzymes—yes, those tiny helpers. These juices get to work breaking down proteins into smaller parts. The stomach's strong muscles churn the food, mixing it with these juices to create a semi-liquid mixture called chyme. This churning action ensures the food is fully exposed to the digestive enzymes and acids, breaking it down into a form your body can later absorb.

Next, the chyme moves into the **small intestine**, where most nutrient absorption happens. The small intestine is a long, coiled tube where the chyme is mixed with bile and digestive enzymes. Bile, created in the liver, helps break down fats into smaller droplets, making them easier to digest. Then, pancreatic enzymes break down our food's three essential so-called macronutrients: **carbohydrates**, **proteins**, and **fats** into their simplest forms—

sugars, amino acids, and fatty acids. The walls of the small intestine are covered with tiny, finger-like projections called villi. These villi help increase the surface area, allowing for more efficient absorption of nutrients. Nutrients pass through these villi and enter the bloodstream, ready to be delivered to cells throughout your body.

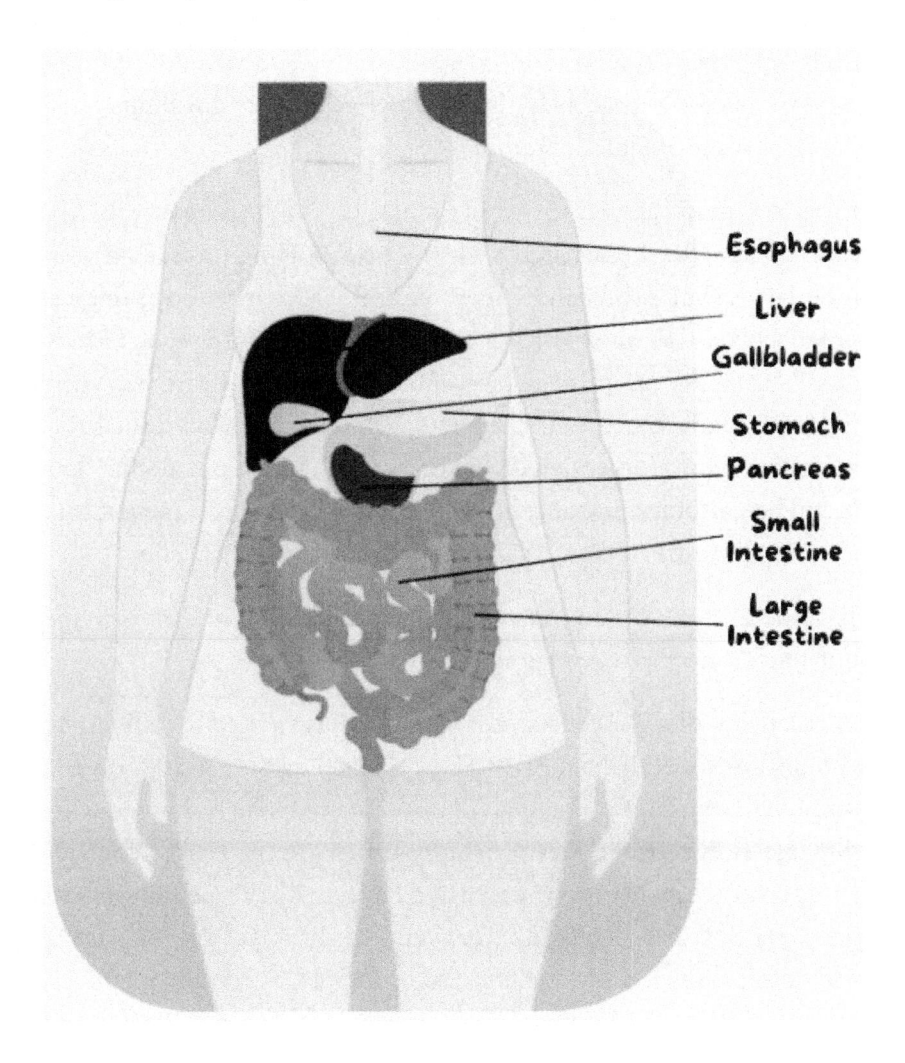

What's left over moves into the **large intestine**, where water and electrolytes are absorbed. The large intestine is shorter and broader than the small intestine and is crucial in forming and storing waste. As water is absorbed, the remaining material becomes more solid, forming stool. This waste is stored in the **rectum** until excreted during a bowel movement. That's the scientific way of describing when somebody is going to the toilet big time… Anyway, the large intestine also houses a diverse community of bacteria that help break down certain substances and produce some essential vitamins.

Every organ in the digestive system has its own important job. The esophagus is like a muscular highway transporting food from your mouth to your stomach. The **liver**, one of your body's largest organs, produces bile, which is crucial for digesting and absorbing fats. The pancreas releases a combination of digestive enzymes into the small intestine. These enzymes help break down the three macronutrients for easier digestion: carbohydrates, proteins, and fats. The **gallbladder** concentrates and stores bile, releasing it into the small intestine when it's needed to help digest fats.

Together, these organs ensure your body gets the energy and nutrients it needs to keep going strong!

A balanced diet is crucial for maintaining a healthy digestive system and overall health. As we explored earlier, our food has three main types of nutrients. All of them are broken down during the digestion process. First, **carbohydrates** are the body's primary energy source, with more extensive contents in foods like bread, pasta, and fruits. They are broken down into simple sugars, providing a quick and efficient energy supply. Secondly, **proteins**, found in meat, beans, and nuts, are essential for building and repairing tissues. Proteins are broken down into amino acids.

Those acids are then used to create new proteins and repair damaged cells.

Lastly, **fats**, typically found in oils, butter, and avocados, support cell function and provide a concentrated energy source. They are broken down into fatty acids and glycerol for energy and building cell membranes.

Vitamins and **minerals** found in various foods regulate numerous body processes, from boosting the immune system to supporting bone health.

For a hands-on learning experience, take your next trip to the supermarket as an opportunity to scan the labels on food packages. Look at the nutritional information and note the different distributions of carbohydrates, proteins, and fats. Reflect on how these nutrients contribute to your diet and overall health. Consider how a balanced diet provides all the essential nutrients by including various foods your body needs to function optimally. This activity will help you understand the importance of making informed food choices and maintaining a balanced diet for a healthy digestive system and overall well-being.

HOW OUR IMMUNE SYSTEM FIGHTS GERMS

Think of your body as a well-guarded fortress, always on alert to defend against tiny invaders like bacteria, viruses, and other harmful pathogens. Standing guard is your immune system, a complex network that protects you from infections and keeps you healthy. The first line of defense is your **skin** and **mucous membranes**. Your skin is a physical barrier, preventing most pathogens from entering your body. Mucous membranes in areas like your nose and mouth produce mucus to trap invaders. This slimy substance catches germs and uses enzymes to break them down, making it harder for them to infect you.

The second line of defense kicks in if pathogens get past these barriers. This includes **white blood cells** and the **inflammatory response**. White blood cells, or leukocytes, patrol your bloodstream and tissues, always looking for foreign invaders. When they detect a pathogen, they release chemicals that cause inflammation. The blood flow in the affected area increases, bringing more white blood cells to fight off the infection. Inflammation often results in redness, heat, swelling, and pain, signaling that your body is defending itself.

The third line of defense involves **antibodies** and **immune memory**. When your immune system encounters a pathogen, it produces antibodies, specialized proteins that recognize and neutralize foreign invaders. These antibodies bind to the pathogens, marking them for destruction by other immune cells. Once your body fights off an infection, it creates memory cells that "remember" the pathogen. If you reencounter the same invader, your immune system can respond more quickly and effectively, often preventing you from getting sick.

The immune response begins with recognition. Your immune cells have receptors that can identify specific molecules called antigens on the surface of pathogens. When a pathogen enters your body, these receptors detect the antigens and sound the alarm. This triggers the response phase, where various immune cells spring into action to attack and destroy the invader. Macrophages, a type of white blood cell, engulf and digest pathogens, acting like the body's cleanup crew. T cells, another kind of white blood cell, attack infected cells directly, destroying them to stop the spread of infection. Meanwhile, B cells produce antibodies that target the pathogen, helping neutralize and prevent it from causing harm.

The memory phase ensures long-term protection after the immediate threat is dealt with. Memory cells remain vigilant, ready to respond rapidly if the same pathogen tries to invade again. This memory is the principle behind vaccinations, which expose your immune system to a harmless form of a pathogen, teaching it to recognize and fight the real thing in the future.

Here are some fun facts about your immune system: First, your body produces about 100 billion white blood cells daily to protect you. Second, laughter can boost your immune system by increasing the production of antibodies and activating T cells. So, having a good laugh isn't just fun—it's good for your health too! Lastly, the immune system is so sophisticated that it can distinguish between thousands of pathogens, ensuring a targeted and effective response every time.

The immune system is an incredible network that tirelessly defends your body from countless threats. From the outer barriers of your skin to the specialized cells inside you, every part works together to keep you healthy and strong. Understanding this system's functions helps us appreciate its complex and vital role in our well-being.

THE SKELETAL SYSTEM: OUR BODY'S FRAMEWORK

Can you imagine your body without bones? You'd be a floppy pile of muscles, organs, and skin, unable to stand, move, or even hold a shape. The skeletal system provides the rigid framework that supports and protects your body, enabling movement and giving you your unique shape. **Bones** are the primary components of this system, acting as the body's structural support. They protect vital organs—the skull shields your brain, and the ribcage guards your heart and lungs. Each bone is a dynamic living tissue that

90 THE SCIENCE FACT BOOK FOR CHILDREN

constantly remodels itself, adapting to stresses and repairing damage.

Joints are where two or more bones meet. They allow for a range of movements, from the hinge-like action of your elbows and knees to the ball-and-socket motion of your shoulders and hips. **Cartilage**, a smooth, rubbery tissue, covers the ends of bones at joints, cushioning them and reducing friction. This cushioning is crucial for soft, pain-free movement. Picture cartilage as the shock absorbers in a car, ensuring a smooth ride. **Ligaments** are strong, fibrous tissues that connect bones to other bones,stabilizing joints and helping control their range of motion. Think of them as the sturdy ropes holding a suspension bridge together, providing strength and flexibility.

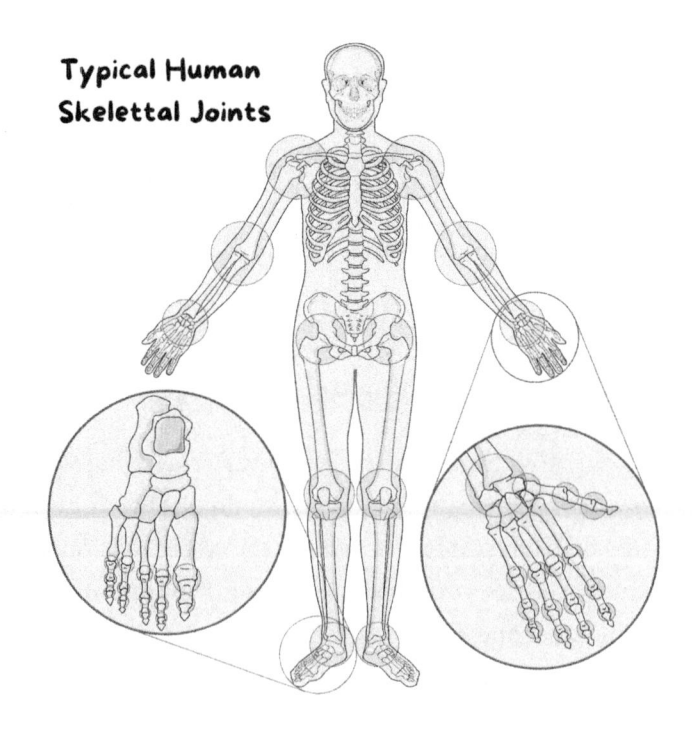

Typical Human Skelettal Joints

Bones come in various shapes and sizes, each designed for specific functions. Long bones, such as the femur in your thigh, provide strength and mobility. They act like levers, enabling powerful movements. Short bones, like the carpals in your wrist, offer stability and facilitate precise movements. These bones are cube shaped, allowing for a range of motions in multiple directions. Flat bones, such as the shoulder blade, protect internal organs and provide surfaces for muscle attachment. These bones are thin and often curved, creating broad surfaces for muscles to attach to. Irregular bones, like the vertebrae in your spine, have complex shapes tailored for specific functions, such as protecting the spinal cord and supporting the body's weight.

Bone growth and repair are fascinating processes. **Ossification** is the process by which a new bone is formed. This occurs in children and adolescents as bones grow and develop, with cartilage gradually replaced by hard bone. In adults, ossification continues, replacing old bone tissue with new tissue. Bone remodeling is a continual process that ensures bones remain strong and can adapt to new stresses. The process relies on the teamwork of osteoclasts, which break down old bone, and osteoblasts, which work to build new bone. This ongoing cycle keeps your skeleton healthy and resilient.

When a bone fractures, the body initiates a remarkable repair process. First, a blood clot forms around the fracture, providing the initial framework for healing. This is followed by forming a soft callus of collagen and cartilage, which gradually hardens into a bony callus. Over time, the bony callus is remodeled, restoring the bone to its original shape. This process can take several weeks to months, depending on the severity of the fracture and the individual's health. When you think about it, it's truly remarkable how the body can heal itself—an incredible phenomenon highlighting one of the key differences between living organisms and mere objects!

Here are some fun facts about bones: First, babies are born with about 300 bones, but by adulthood, humans have only 206. This is because many of the bones fuse together as they grow. Second, the smallest bone in your body is the stapes in the middle ear. It's about the size of a grain of rice and plays a crucial role in hearing by transmitting sound vibrations to the inner ear.

The skeletal system is a marvel of engineering, providing the structure and support that make movement and protection possible. Each bone, joint, and ligament is vital in keeping your body functional and robust. Understanding this system's intricacies highlights the human body's incredible design and adaptability.

THE SCIENCE OF SLEEP: WHY WE NEED IT

Sleep is more than just a nightly ritual; it's a critical pillar of health, affecting every aspect of our well-being. Adequate sleep is crucial for physical health, body repair, and tissue growth. While sleeping, cells' regeneration occurs, aiding in muscle repair as growth hormones are released. This is why athletes and growing children need plenty of rest. Sleep also plays a vital role in supporting **mental health** by processing emotions and solidifying memories. During sleep, your brain sorts through and organizes information from the day, making remembering facts and experiences easier. This mental housekeeping is essential for managing stress and maintaining **emotional balance**.

Cognitive function also benefits immensely from a good night's sleep. You can focus, solve problems, and make better decisions when being well-rested. Else, quickly, you feel foggy and less sharp. It is like solving a puzzle with missing pieces; that's what it's like to think about things with insufficient sleep. Your brain needs rest to function at its best, whether you're studying for an exam, working on a project, or making everyday decisions.

Establishing good sleep hygiene can significantly improve the quality of your rest.

Maintaining a consistent **sleep schedule** is a great way to improve your sleep. Aim to go to bed and wake up at the same time every day, including weekends, to establish a consistent routine. Sticking to the same weekly schedule helps your body maintain a natural rhythm, making it easier to wake up without feeling groggy. This regular routine helps keep your internal clock, or circadian rhythm, in sync. Over time, your body will know when to wind down for the night.

Along with a steady schedule, creating a comfortable, quiet, and relaxing **sleep environment** is just as important. A peaceful setting signals to your body that it's time to rest, setting the stage for deep, restful sleep. Ensure your bedroom is cool, dark, and calm. Consider blackout curtains, earplugs, or a white noise machine if you live in a noisy area. Your bed should be a place of comfort, with a mattress that provides the proper support for your body and pillows that match your preferred sleeping position, ensuring you wake up feeling refreshed and free of aches.

Limiting screen time before bed is another crucial part of maintaining good sleep hygiene. Digital devices like smartphones and tablets emit blue light, which can trick your brain into thinking it's still daytime, reducing the production of melatonin—the hormone that signals to your body it's time to sleep. To help your body wind down, avoid using such screens for at least an hour before you go to bed. Instead of scrolling through your phone, consider calming activities that promote relaxation, like reading a favorite book, taking a warm bath, or practicing deep breathing or meditation. These soothing habits signal to your body that it's time to rest and can make falling asleep much easier.

Sleep consists of two distinct phases, each essential for rest and recovery. These phases are called REM sleep and non-REM sleep, and together, they form the natural sleep cycle that our bodies go through each night. Each phase has its unique purpose, contributing to mental and physical restoration.

Non-REM sleep consists of three stages. The first stage is light sleep, where you drift in and out of consciousness. The second stage is a deeper sleep, where your heart rate slows and your body temperature drops. Deep sleep, called slow-wave sleep, is the third step, where the body repairs tissues and strengthens the immune system. **REM sleep** is the dreaming phase, characterized by rapid eye movements and increased brain activity. This stage is crucial for emotional processing and memory consolidation.

Keep a sleep diary for one or two weeks to explore your sleep patterns. Record what time you go to bed, wake up, and how you feel in the morning. Note any daytime sleepiness, energy levels throughout the day, and any naps you take. This exercise can help you identify patterns and areas for improvement. Additionally, observe the effects of screen time on your sleep. Track how much screen time you consume in the evenings, particularly in the last hour before bed. Note how long it takes to fall asleep after ending screen use. Reflect on any differences in the quality of your sleep and how you feel the next day.

In essence, sleep is a vital component of health, affecting physical repair, mental well-being, and cognitive function. By establishing healthy sleep habits and understanding the importance of each sleep stage, you can improve your overall quality of life. As we wrap up our exploration of the human body, remember that each system plays a unique and indispensable role in keeping you healthy and thriving.

Next, we'll venture into the world of physics, uncovering the principles that govern our everyday lives. From the force of gravity that keeps us grounded to the invisible magnetism that powers our devices, physics helps us understand the fundamental workings of the universe.

If Learning Is So Crucial, Why Do We Still Make It So Boring?

"Education is the most powerful weapon you can use to change the world."

BB KING

Remember the good old days of school? Textbooks, blackboards, and endless copying of notes followed by exams that had enough power to determine our future. It was far from interesting or fun and if we are perfectly honest, not much actually stuck in our minds.

Things are improving. As technology continues to advance, the classroom is becoming more interactive. But it's still almost impossible for teachers to be able to cater to the needs of each child in a classroom and this means more and more parents, grandparents, and extended family members are getting involved with children's education.

But that's no easy task. First, adults might be lacking knowledge, and more importantly, how on earth do you engage children when the thought of more learning is just boring for them?

By now, you will have noticed that fun facts and snippets of information integrated into their day are one of the best ways of capturing the attention and enthusiasm of these eager minds.

Whether it's geothermal energy, the superpowers of animals, or the mysteries of space, the children in your life are soaking up information that will truly benefit them, from discovering more about their interests to gaining academic confidence.

Unfortunately, not all adults are in the same position and this means there are so many children that are still struggling with their learning and dreading school.

It doesn't have to be this way for the children, nor for the adults who desperately want to help them. Just a few words from you can help them discover the effectiveness of fun facts.

A few words on Amazon, sharing your opinions of this book are all it takes for the next person to be able to take an active role in a child's education and enjoy some jaw-dropping facts at the same time.

I know you are busy and have a ton of responsibilities so I have kept the process quick and simple. With just a couple of clicks and a few minutes, I am confident that we can help more children approach learning with a new perspective!

Scan the QR code below

CHAPTER FIVE
PHYSICS IN EVERYDAY LIFE

Picture this: you're standing in line for the roller coaster at a theme park. The anticipation builds as the coaster climbs to the top of the first hill. Suddenly, it plummets down, and you feel your stomach drop as you speed toward the ground. That thrilling sensation you experience is all thanks to gravity, the invisible force that keeps us grounded and makes roller coasters so exciting. But **Gravity** does much more than create fun rides—it's a fundamental force that shapes our very existence. One of the many facts to discover from the science of physics, like **Simple Machines**, **Magnetism**, **Electricity**, **Sound**, and **Light**, to count a few, which we will cover in this chapter.

GRAVITY: WHY WE DON'T FLOAT AWAY

Gravity is the **force** that pulls objects toward one another. **Isaac Newton**, one of the most renowned scientists in history, developed the law of universal gravitation to explain how this force works. According to Newton, every object with mass attracts every other object with mass. The strength of this pull depends on both the masses of the objects and the distance between them.

While we're keeping things simple and avoiding formulas in this book, it's important to note that as the distance between two objects increases, the gravitational attraction between them decreases.

Legend has it that Newton was inspired to develop his many theories—including the one about gravity—when he was strolling around an apple tree at Woolsthorpe Manor in the UK and noticed an apple falling to the ground. While a lot has been written about the tree incident and whether it happened, we can definitely say that, on Earth, gravity pulls everything—including apples—toward the planet's center.

This is why you stay firmly planted on the ground instead of floating into space. The Earth's gravitational pull is what gives you weight. Imagine jumping off a diving board—gravity pulls you down into the water. Without gravity, you'd just float away, and diving would be much less fun!

Gravity affects objects of different masses in fascinating ways. One of the most famous experiments demonstrating this was conducted by **Galileo Galilei**. According to another legend, Galileo dropped two objects of different weights from the Leaning Tower of Pisa in Italy to show that they fell at the same rate, landing simultaneously on the ground. This experiment disproved the long-held belief that heavier objects fall faster than lighter ones. Galileo's findings revealed that due to gravity, with air resistance being absent, **all objects fall with the same acceleration**, regardless of their mass. Accordingly, a feather only falls slower than a stone because its shape creates a lot of air resistance.

The difference between mass and weight is an important concept to grasp. **Mass** is the amount of matter in an object, which remains constant no matter where you are in the universe. Whether on Earth, on the Moon, or floating in deep space, your mass stays the same. **Weight**, on the other hand, is the force exerted by gravity on that mass. Your weight can change depending on the strength of the gravitational pull. For example, you would weigh less on the Moon than on Earth because the Moon's gravity is weaker.

To see gravity in action, try this simple experiment. Take two objects of similar size but significantly different weights, like a cube of sugar and a stone. Go outside and drop them from the same height. Observe how they fall. You'll notice that they hit the ground at the same time, demonstrating that gravity accelerates all objects equally, regardless of their mass. This experiment is a great way to visualize one of Galileo's key discoveries.

Gravity is a fundamental force that shapes our world in countless ways. It's why you can enjoy thrilling roller coaster rides, jump off diving boards, and walk on the ground. Understanding gravity helps us appreciate the invisible forces that govern our everyday lives. So, the next time you're at a theme park or simply dropping a sugar cube into your tea, remember the incredible power of gravity at work.

SIMPLE MACHINES: MAKING WORK EASIER

Imagine you're trying to lift a heavy box onto a high shelf. You could struggle and strain or use a lever, one of the simplest yet most ingenious tools created by humans. Simple machines have little to no moving parts but help make tasks easier by increasing or changing the direction of the force you apply. They include levers, wheels and axles, pulleys, inclined planes, wedges, and screws. These tools reduce the effort needed to perform tasks by providing mechanical advantage, which allows a smaller force to move a larger load over a greater distance.

Levers are everywhere, from seesaws in playgrounds to crowbars used for prying open stuck objects. A lever is a rigid bar that pivots around a fixed point called the fulcrum. When you apply force on one end, the lever amplifies this force, making it easier to lift or move an object on the other end. Next time you use a bottle opener, you'll use a lever to pry off the cap with minimal effort. The same principle applies to scissors, which have two levers working together to cut through paper or fabric.

Wheels and axles are another type of simple machine that makes transportation and movement much easier. Take a bicycle, for example: The wheels reduce friction, allowing you to glide smoothly over different surfaces. The axle connects the wheels and transfers the force from the pedals to the wheels, pushing you forward. Rolling carts, office chairs, and even your suitcase at the airport all rely on wheels and axles to easily move heavy loads. So, the next time you roll your suitcase through the airport, thank the wheel and axle for making your journey smoother!

Pulleys are indispensable for lifting heavy objects. A pulley consists of a wheel with a groove around its edge through which a rope or cable runs. When you pull on one end of the rope in a pulley system, the pulley changes the direction of your pull and can make it easier to lift. If the pulley is set up so that you pull the rope a longer distance than the actual height at which the load needs to be lifted, the effort required is much less. It's like trading more distance for less strength, letting you lift something heavy without needing as much muscle power. You can find pulleys in flagpoles, where they help raise and lower flags, and in cranes at construction sites, where they lift heavy building materials. By using multiple pulleys in a system known as a **block and tackle**, you can significantly reduce the effort needed to lift heavy objects.

Inclined planes are simple machines that allow you to move objects up or down a slope with less effort. A ramp is a perfect example. Instead of lifting a heavy box straight up, you can push it up a ramp, spreading the effort over a longer distance. Slides in playgrounds and loading ramps for trucks use inclined planes to make tasks easier. By reducing the force needed to lift an object, inclined planes make moving heavy loads more manageable.

Wedges can be used to split or cut objects apart. A wedge consists of two inclined planes joined together, forming a sharp edge. When you apply force to the thick end, the wedge drives into an object, splitting it apart. Axes and knives are typical examples of wedges. When you chop wood with an axe or slice bread with a knife, you use a wedge to apply force more effectively. Doorstops and chisels are other everyday tools that utilize the power of wedges.

Screws are inclined planes wrapped around a cylinder, creating a spiral shape that converts rotational force into linear motion. When you turn a screw, the threads pull the screw into the material, holding things together tightly. Jar lids, bolts, and car jacks are all examples of screws in action. The next time you open a jar of pickles, think about how the screw mechanism makes it possible to seal and unseal the jar with ease.

SIMPLE MACHINES

Pulley

Lever

Wheel and Axle

Wedge

Inclined Plane

Screw

PHYSICS IN EVERYDAY LIFE   105

Simple machines are integral to our daily lives, making tasks easier and more efficient. Scissors, for instance, use levers to cut through materials with minimal effort. Screws hold together furniture and appliances, ensuring they stay sturdy and functional. In construction and engineering, pulleys help lift heavy materials, and inclined planes allow workers to move loads safely and efficiently. Simple machines are often the building blocks of more complex machinery, demonstrating the power of fundamental principles in solving everyday challenges.

For a hands-on observation activity, visit a construction site and observe the main elements of a crane. Notice how the crane uses counterweights and levers to balance and lift heavy loads. Reflect on the physics at play and how simple machines make such impressive feats possible.

You may also take a closer look at your bicycle. Observe why the pedal wheel is typically bigger than the driven wheel. Consider how different gears affect the force needed to pedal and the bike's speed. These observations will deepen your understanding and appreciation of simple machines and their practical applications.

MAGNETISM: INVISIBLE FORCES AT WORK

You're using a compass to find your way during a hike, and the needle swings around until it points north. That's the magic of magnets in action! Magnets are amazing objects that create invisible lines of force called **magnetic fields**. These fields are strongest at the magnet's ends, known as the north and south poles. When you bring two magnets near each other, you'll notice that opposite poles attract (north to south), while like poles push each other away (north to north or south to south). This simple yet powerful interaction is the essence of magnetism. It plays a huge role in everyday life, from guiding explorers to helping your headphones work!

Materials with natural magnetism, known as **ferromagnetic** materials, can generate magnetic fields without any external force. Examples include iron, nickel, and cobalt, which contain aligned magnetic domains that create a persistent magnetic field. These materials are the foundation for our everyday magnets, from refrigerator magnets to the internal components of electric motors.

The relationship between electricity and magnetism is captivating and fundamental to modern technology. When an electric current flows through a wire, it generates a magnetic field around it. This phenomenon is the principle behind **electromagnets**, magnets created by electricity. By wrapping a coil of wire around an iron core and passing an electric current through it, you can make a powerful magnet. This principle, known as electromagnetism, was discovered by **Michael Faraday**. Faraday's law of induction describes how a changing magnetic field can generate an electric current in a conductor. This discovery paved the way for electric generators, transformers, and other devices that power our world.

You encounter magnetism in numerous everyday situations. Take the magnetic compass, a tool used for centuries for navigation. Compasses work by aligning with the Earth's magnetic field, helping explorers navigate and stay on course with the help of maps.

Fun fact: Not all planets have a magnetic field! Our neighboring planets, Venus and Mars, lack this feature, making Earth's magnetic field unique. It not only guides explorers but also protects us from harmful radiation in space, acting like a shield for our planet.

In more advanced applications, magnetic levitation (maglev) trains use powerful electromagnets to float above the tracks, reducing friction and enabling incredibly smooth and fast travel.

Ferrofluids are an intriguing example of magnetism that you might not see daily. These unique liquids contain tiny magnetic particles suspended in a carrier fluid. Ferrofluids exhibit striking behaviors when exposed to a magnetic field, forming spikes and patterns along the field lines. These fluids are used in various applications, from sealing and cooling hard drives to creating dynamic art installations. The fascinating properties of ferrofluids showcase the versatility and beauty of magnetic phenomena.

To explore magnetism firsthand, try a simple experiment with household magnets. Gather various magnets and test their attraction and repulsion on different surfaces. See where they stick and where they don't. This activity will help you understand the nature of magnetic fields and how they interact with various materials. Another engaging activity is to go on a nature walk to find naturally occurring magnetic rocks, such as magnetite. These rocks are often found in areas with volcanic activity or near old mining sites. Bring a small magnet along to test whether it sticks to the stones you find. This hands-on exploration will deepen your appreciation for the natural presence of magnetism.

Understanding magnetism opens the door to a world of invisible forces that shape our everyday experiences. From the simple act of sticking a note on the fridge to the advanced technology of maglev trains, magnetism plays a crucial role in our lives. By exploring these concepts and conducting experiments, you can uncover the fascinating principles that govern the magnetic forces around us.

THE BASICS OF ELECTRICITY: POWERING OUR WORLD

Electricity is the heartbeat of modern life. It powers your smartphone, lights up your home, and even makes your toaster pop out that perfect slice of toast in the morning. But what exactly is electricity? At its core, it's the flow of tiny particles called **electrons**, moving through a conductor like a metal wire. This movement is what we call an **electric current**. You can think of it like a river of electrons, steadily flowing from one place to another. **Voltage**, on the other hand, is like the force that pushes this river along—it's the electric potential difference between two points that gets those electrons moving. Using the river as a reference, the voltage would compare to the height difference at two locations, leading the water to flow down. **Conductors**, such as copper, silver, and aluminum, are like open highways for electricity, allowing it to flow easily. Meanwhile, **insulators**, like rubber and glass, act as barriers, keeping the electricity contained.

There are two types of electric current: **Direct Current (DC)** and **Alternating Current (AC)**. DC flows in one direction, like a steady stream. Batteries provide DC, which is perfect for powering small devices like flashlights and remote controls. AC, on the other hand, changes direction periodically, like the tide ebbing and flowing. This is the type of current that powers your home. It's generated by power plants and can be easily transmitted at more significant amounts over long distances, which is why it's used for the electrical grid. AC can be converted to different voltages using transformers, making it versatile and efficient for large-scale power distribution.

Electricity can be generated in various ways. We touched on this in the renewable energy section of the engineering chapter. To produce electricity, traditional power plants burn fossil fuels like coal, oil, and natural gas. These fuels are burned to heat water, creating steam that connects turbines to generators. Those can be connected to wind turbines or water dams, which similarly generate electricity. Alternatively, solar panels convert sunlight directly into electricity using photovoltaic cells.

Pathways through which electricity flows are called **electrical circuits**. A basic circuit consists of a power source, such as a battery, connected to various components like resistors, switches, and bulbs. Series and parallel circuits are the two main types of circuits. In a series circuit, all the elements are connected one after another, so the same current flows through each one. The downside? If one component stops working, the entire circuit is broken, and everything shuts down. On the other hand, in a parallel circuit, components are connected across common points, creating multiple paths for the current to flow. This means that if one path fails, the current can still flow through the others, making parallel circuits more reliable in most situations.

An everyday example of a parallel circuit is the wiring in your home. Imagine turning on a light in a room with more than one switch. Suppose the electrician had wired it as a series circuit. In that case, you'd have to ensure every switch was in the correct position to turn on the light—talk about frustrating! But thanks to the parallel arrangement, you can easily turn the light on at one switch and off at another, making it super convenient. And the next time you want to turn it on, you can use either switch without a hassle. However, some electrical applications may require series circuits for safety or other technical reasons.

One way to observe electricity in action is by noticing static electricity in your daily life. Have you ever rubbed a balloon on your hair and watched it stick to the wall? That's static electricity at work. Pay attention to the static shocks you might feel when touching a doorknob after walking on a carpet. These shocks occur because of the buildup and sudden discharge of static electricity. This is due to an existing voltage between you and the doorknob, which physicists also may refer to as a potential difference. Reflect on how and why these events happen, and you'll better understand their principles.

Another fascinating activity is observing the power of lightning during a thunderstorm. While thunderstorms can be intense, they offer a spectacular display of natural electricity. Watch lightning from a safe distance, ideally indoors. Notice the bright flashes and the sound of thunder that follows. Reflect on how lightning is a giant static discharge, similar to the small shocks you experience but on a much grander scale. The energy released by a single lightning bolt is immense, showcasing the raw power of electricity in nature. And be aware that it can be pretty dangerous; hence, please adhere to some safety rules in such situations.

Safety should be your top priority when you're outside and a thunderstorm rolls in. Here are some important rules to keep in mind:

1. **Seek Shelter Immediately**: When you hear thunder, find a safe place to shelter. Your best bet is a sturdy building or a car with a metal roof. Avoid small shelters like tents or pavilions, as they won't offer enough protection.
2. **Avoid Tall Objects**: Lightning tends to strike the tallest object around, so stay away from trees, poles, and open fields. If you're caught in an open area, crouch down low with your feet together, minimizing your contact with the ground, but don't lie flat.
3. **Stay Away From Water**: Water is a great conductor of electricity, so stay out of lakes, rivers, and pools during a storm. If you're boating or swimming, get to land as quickly as possible.
4. **Don't Use Metal Objects**: Metal attracts lightning, so avoid using or carrying metal objects like umbrellas, golf clubs, or bicycles. If you're wearing metal jewelry, it's best to take it off until the storm passes.
5. **Wait It Out**: Even after the thunder seems to have stopped, wait at least 30 minutes before leaving your shelter. Lightning can strike even when the storm appears to be moving away.

Lightning Safety Tips (Outdoor)

- Struck by lightning
- Avoid motors (machinery)
- Avoid high ground
- Do not swim
- Do not fly kite
- Find shelter in building (not canopy)
- Do not stand under tall objects
- Do not carry an umbrella
- Get inside a car
- Crouching down and cover ears (if outside)
- Avoid open areas

Remember, thunderstorms can be dangerous, but by following these safety rules, you can protect yourself and stay out of harm's way. As we wrap up this electricity section, remember that the flow of energy in the shape of electricity is all around us and powers our daily lives, from the simplest light switch to the most complex machines. It's a force that sparks innovation and keeps our modern world connected.

THE SCIENCE OF SOUND: HOW WE HEAR

Imagine you're at a concert or watching a movie with a modern-day surround system, feeling the bass thump in your chest and the sounds swirling around you. That's sound in action, making its way through the air to reach your ears. Sound is created by **vibrations** sending waves through a medium, whether air, water, or even a solid object. Its velocity changes depending on the medium. As a matter of fact, in water, sound travels more than four times faster than in air. The mentioned wave vibrations push and pull on the particles around them, setting off a chain reaction. These movements create ripples, known as **sound waves**. These sound waves travel in the air as compressions and rarefactions—areas where air molecules are pushed together and then spread apart. These waves carry energy from the source of the sound to your ears, allowing you to hear everything from the softest whisper to the roar of a powerful engine.

The human ear is an incredible organ that captures, amplifies, and translates these sound waves into signals our brains can understand. The **outer ear**, which includes the visible part called the pinna and the ear canal, acts like a funnel, capturing sound waves and directing them inward. When these waves reach the eardrum, a thin membrane that vibrates in response to sound, they start a chain reaction in the **middle ear**. The middle ear contains three tiny bones—the hammer, anvil, and stirrup—that amplify the vibrations and transmit them to the inner ear.

The magic happens in the **inner ear**, where we find the cochlea, a spiral-shaped organ lined with tiny hair cells and filled with fluid. When the vibrations reach the cochlea, they create waves in the fluid, moving the hair cells. These movements generate electrical signals that are transmitted to our brain. There, these signals are interpreted as sound, allowing you to hear music, voices, and all the other noises that make up our auditory world.

Sound has several fundamental properties, including pitch, volume, and frequency. **Pitch** is determined by the **frequency** of sound waves—the number of waves that pass a point in one second. High-frequency waves produce high-pitched sounds, like a whistle, while low-frequency waves produce low-pitched sounds, like a drum. On the other hand, **volume** is determined by the amplitude of the sound waves—the height of the waves. Larger amplitudes create louder sounds, while smaller amplitudes create softer sounds.

To truly appreciate the richness of sound, spend time in different outdoor environments and listen to nature's soundscapes. Sit quietly in a park, forest, or stream and identify the various sound sources. Notice how birds chirping, leaves rustling, and water babbling create a symphony of natural noises. Reflect on how these sounds make you feel and what they tell you about your surroundings. This activity helps you connect with the natural world and enhances your listening ability.

Another fascinating way to explore sound is by observing echoes in everyday life. Find locations where echoes are common, such as empty rooms, hallways, or canyons. Clap your hands and listen for the returning sound. An echo occurs when sound waves bounce off a surface and travel back to your ears. The time it takes for the echo to return depends on the distance of the reflecting surface. Pay attention to how the echo changes with different surfaces and distances. This activity helps you understand how sound waves interact with their environment and provides a fun way to experience the science of sound firsthand.

LIGHT AND OPTICS: HOW WE SEE

Imagine stepping outside on a bright, sunny day. The warmth you feel and the world you see is thanks to **light**. It's a type of energy that travels in **waves** but sometimes behaves like a **particle**, a dual nature that has puzzled scientists for centuries. It all depends on the kind of experiment conducted to uncover its nuances. But what exactly is light?

Light, the essence of vision, is another marvel of physics. Scientists would say that light is a form of **electromagnetic radiation** that allows us to see everything around us. It moves incredibly fast, bouncing off objects and traveling to our eyes, where it's turned into the images we see. When you see a rainbow or the sparkle of sunlight on water, you're witnessing light's wave behavior. As a wave, light travels at an incredible speed of approximately 300000 kilometers per second in a vacuum—about one billion kilometers per hour or nearly 670 million miles per hour. However, this speed changes when light passes through different mediums like water or glass, slowing down and bending in a process called **refraction**.

Now, let's explore how we see the world around us. Your eyes are intricate organs designed to capture and convert light into images. When light enters the **eye**, it first passes through the cornea, a transparent, curved surface that helps focus the light. The light then travels through the lens, fine-tuning the focus and directing the light onto the retina at the back of the eye. The retina is a layer of light-sensitive cells that convert the light into electrical signals. These signals travel along the optic nerve to the brain, where they are interpreted as visual images. It's a seamless process that happens literally in the blink of an eye!

Light behaves in fascinating ways, creating various optical phenomena we encounter daily. **Reflection** is when sunlight bounces off a surface, like seeing your face in a mirror or on a water surface, depending on the conditions.

The angle at which the light hits the surface determines the angle at which it reflects, following the law of reflection. Refraction, on the other hand, occurs when light passes from one medium to another, like from air to water, causing it to bend. This bending effect is why a straw looks bent when you see it in a glass of water. **Dispersion** is another captivating phenomenon, where light splits into its component colors, creating a spectrum. A classic example of dispersion is a prism splitting white light into a rainbow of colors.

Try watching shadows throughout the day to observe the wonders of light and shadow. Notice how the length and direction of shadows change as the Sun moves across the sky. In the morning and late afternoon, shadows are long and stretch away from the Sun. At noon, when the Sun is directly overhead, shadows are short and directly beneath objects. This activity helps you see how the position of a light source affects the shadows it casts, providing a hands-on understanding of light behavior.

Another engaging activity is exploring reflections in everyday objects. Look at your reflection in mirrors, windows, water puddles, or shiny surfaces. Observe how clear or distorted your reflection appears depending on the surface's properties. For instance, a smooth, polished mirror provides a clear reflection, while a rippling water surface creates a wavy, distorted image. This activity allows you to see the principles of reflection in action and understand how different surfaces affect how light behaves.

By understanding the nature of light and the workings of the human eye, you gain a deeper appreciation for the incredible process of vision. The phenomena of reflection, refraction, and dispersion reveal the complexity and beauty of light, enriching your perception of the world around you. As you explore these concepts, remember that light is not just something that illuminates our surroundings—it's a fundamental aspect of how we experience and interpret reality.

You may have noticed that I have steered clear of any complicated formulas. But here's something to reflect on whenever there is news citing famous scientific journals like, for instance, *Nature*: One of the many exciting jobs of a physicist is to develop theories and mathematical models that predict how things will behave, whether it's the pull of gravity, the power of magnetism, the flow of electricity, or even the motion of planets and stars. When scientists see their predictions come true, it's like cracking a secret code of the universe—a moment of deep satisfaction and triumph. So, while we didn't dive into complex formulas, remember that behind every discovery, there's a scientist thrilled to see their work come to life!

Next, we'll delve into chemistry, exploring the building blocks of matter and the reactions that create the world around us.

CHAPTER SIX
CHEMISTRY AROUND US

Have you ever wondered what makes up everything around you, from the air we breathe to the food we eat? It all comes down to **atoms and molecules**, the tiny building blocks of matter. It is a fascinating world about the smallest units of matter that make up the universe. In this chapter, we'll explore how these particles come together to form everything in our world and how scientists organize them into the **Periodic Table**, a powerful tool for understanding the elements. We'll also dive into the exciting world of **chemical reactions**, where substances change and transform, heading over to cover **acids and bases** and why some things taste sour or feel slippery. Plus, we'll explore **polymers**, which make up the plastics we use daily, and the **chemistry of cooking**, showing how heat changes food at a molecular level. Welcome to the fascinating chemistry all around us!

ATOMS AND MOLECULES: THE BUILDING BLOCKS OF MATTER

Atoms are the smallest units of an **element**, like a single piece of a gigantic cosmic jigsaw puzzle. Now, you may have heard about more minor components, but atoms are the most minor units that still retain the chemical properties of that element. An element is a pure substance comprising only one type of atom, like oxygen or gold, and we will learn more about them in the next section. But first, we continue to dissect and understand atoms.

Each atom consists of a **nucleus**, which is like the dense core of a tiny solar system. The nucleus is packed with **protons** and **neutrons**. Protons carry a positive charge, while neutrons are neutral, having no charge at all. This dense nucleus is surrounded by a swirling cloud of **electrons**—negatively charged particles that orbit the nucleus at various energy levels.

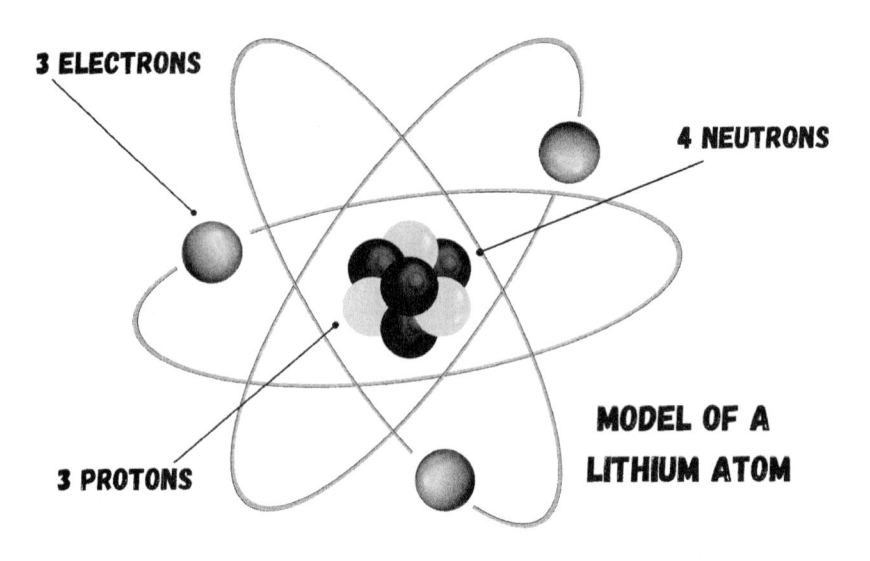

3 ELECTRONS

4 NEUTRONS

3 PROTONS

MODEL OF A LITHIUM ATOM

These electrons are much smaller than protons and neutrons—about 1800 times smaller, in fact! Hence, in most illustrations, electrons are drawn much more extensively than they would be compared to the core.

Now, let's talk about what happens when atoms join forces. When two or more atoms bond, they form molecules, the smallest units of a chemical compound. A molecule can be as simple as oxygen gas, which we breathe, or as complex as DNA, the blueprint of life. The way atoms bond together to form molecules can be understood through different types of chemical bonds: covalent bonds and ionic bonds.

Covalent bonds occur when atoms share electrons. Imagine you and a friend both having a snack, but instead of keeping them to yourselves, you decide to **share** them. This sharing creates a bond that holds the atoms together. Water is a classic example of covalent bonding with hydrogen and oxygen atoms involved. Each hydrogen atom shares an electron with the oxygen atom, forming a molecule that is essential for life.

A second example is carbon dioxide, another critical molecule. It has a carbon atom in the center, flanked by two oxygen atoms on either side. This molecule is generated by many processes converting energy, be it combustion or human breath. We discussed carbon dioxide in the biology chapter; plants use it during photosynthesis to create oxygen and glucose, which are vital for sustaining life on Earth.

On the other hand, **ionic bonds** form when one atom actually **transfers** an electron to another. Instead of sharing the snack we mentioned, you and your friend give it to someone else. Table salt, involving the atoms of sodium and chlorine, is a perfect example of an ionic bond. Sodium donates an electron to chlorine, resulting in a molecule that we sprinkle on our food every day.

Atoms and molecules are at the heart of everything, from the air we breathe to the food we eat. Understanding their structure and how they bond together gives us a more profound appreciation for the natural world. The next time you sip water or season your food with salt, remember the incredible chemistry at play, making life as we know it possible.

THE PERIODIC TABLE: ORGANIZING THE ELEMENTS

Imagine entering a library where every book is perfectly arranged, making it easy to find precisely what you're looking for. Now, picture the **periodic table of elements** as that library, but instead of books, it's filled with the basic building blocks of everything around us—elements! Each component is a unique type of atom, and the periodic table is like the ultimate guide, organizing them all based on their properties.

As you move across a row, or period, from left to right, the **atomic number**—basically the number of protons in an element's nucleus—increases. This atomic number is like the element's ID card; it makes each element special and helps determine where it belongs on the table.

The table is set up like a grid, with rows called periods and columns called groups. The cool thing is that an element's spot on this grid tells you a ton about what it's like.

The elements in the same group or column share similar properties. For instance, alkali metals like sodium and potassium are found in the first column. These metals are highly reactive, especially with water, and have a single electron in their outermost shell. This makes them eager to form bonds and participate in chemical reactions. Move over to the 17th column, and you'll find halogens like chlorine and fluorine. These nonmetals are also very reactive but in a different way. They have seven electrons in their outer shell. They are desperate to gain one more to complete it, making them excellent at forming compounds, especially salts.

On the far right of the table, you'll encounter the noble gases, including helium and neon. These elements are like the introverts of the periodic table—completely inert and unreactive. They have full electron shells, making them stable and unlikely to form compounds under normal conditions. This stability is why helium is used in balloons and neon in bright, flashy signs. These distinct group properties help scientists predict how elements will behave in different situations, making the periodic table an invaluable tool in chemistry.

Periodic Table with Elements 1-20

Groups	1	2	13*)	14	15	16	17	18
Period								
1	1 **H** hydrogen 1.01							2 **He** helium 4.00
2	3 **Li** lithium 6.94	4 **Be** beryllium 9.01	5 **B** boron 10.81	6 **C** carbon 12.01	7 **N** nitrogen 14.01	8 **O** oxygen 16.00	9 **F** fluorine 19.00	10 **Ne** neon 20.18
3	11 **Na** sodium 22.99	12 **Mg** magnesium 24.31	13 **Al** aluminum 26.98	14 **Si** silicon 28.09	15 **P** phosphorus 30.97	16 **S** sulfur 32.07	17 **Cl** chlorine 35.45	18 **Ar** argon 39.95
4	19 **K** potassium 39.10	20 **Ca** calcium 40.08	*) From the first 20 elements there are none in groups 3 to 12					

Legend:

3 **Li** lithium 6.94	Atomic number (Number of protons in the atom's nucleus) Symbol (element abbreviation) Element name Atomic mass (average mass of the elements atoms)

Alloys are another fascinating aspect of chemistry, particularly in engineering. An alloy is a mixture of metals designed to have specific properties. For example, steel is an alloy of iron and carbon. It's much stronger than pure iron and is used in everything from skyscrapers to kitchen knives. Bronze, a warm, golden-brown alloy made from copper and tin, has been admired for its durability and resistance to corrosion. With its rich, gleaming surface, this sturdy metal has been used for over 5,000 years to create statues, medals, and countless other items that stand the test of time. These alloys are crucial in mechanical engineering, where materials must withstand stress and wear while allowing to get and maintain very accurate and durable shapes through machining or welding operations.

In electrical engineering and electronics, certain elements and alloys are indispensable. Copper, for instance, is widely used for electrical wiring because of its excellent conductivity. Silicon, a metalloid, is the backbone of the semiconductor industry. It's used to make computer chips that power almost every electronic device you can think of. When found in nature, silicon often appears as a dull gray or brown crystalline solid. It's usually found in the form of sand, quartz, or rock, shimmering slightly in sunlight due to its crystalline structure. In its pure form, silicon has a metallic luster, almost like a shiny piece of rock with a smooth, slightly glassy surface. You might find it embedded in the Earth, where it combines with oxygen to form silicates, making up a large part of its crust and giving rocks and minerals their sturdy, glittering appearance. Alloys like solder, a mix of tin and lead, join electronic components together. These materials are carefully chosen for their specific properties, ensuring that our gadgets and machines work efficiently and reliably.

Try a periodic table scavenger hunt to make learning about the periodic table even more engaging. Look around your home and find items that contain different elements. For instance, your table salt comprises sodium (Na) and chlorine (Cl). The aluminum (Al) foil in your kitchen and the copper (Cu) wires in your electronics are other great examples. Use an internet image search to gather a simple periodic table and print it when possible. Each time you find an item, locate its elements on the periodic table and note their properties. This activity helps you see where all these chemical building blocks form our surrounding world. Alternatively, if car nameplates in your country contain letters, look out for them on long car journeys and make it an exercise or family competition to relate those letters you encounter to as many chemical elements as possible.

The periodic table is more than just a chart; it's a map that guides us through the complex chemistry landscape. It reveals patterns and relationships among elements, helping scientists and engineers create new materials and understand natural phenomena. Every element has a story to tell, and the periodic table is where those stories come together, providing a comprehensive picture of the building blocks of our universe. From the food scientist to the car design engineer to the astrophysicist investigating the composition of faraway space objects, they all have to have basic knowledge of the chemical elements and how to deal with the periodic table.

CHEMICAL REACTIONS: HOW SUBSTANCES CHANGE

Chemical reactions are fascinating processes that transform substances into entirely new ones, mixing and jiggling with chemical elements and molecules. Picture baking a cake. You start with ingredients like flour, sugar, eggs, and baking powder—these are your **reactants** containing the following elements: carbon, hydrogen, oxygen, nitrogen, calcium, and some others. When you mix them and bake the batter, a series of chemical reactions occur, producing a delicious cake called the **product**. In every chemical reaction, the substances you start with, called reactants, change into new substances called products. One fundamental principle of chemistry is the **conservation of mass**. This means matter is neither created nor destroyed during a chemical reaction—in a closed system. The total mass of the reactants equals the total mass of the products, even if they seem entirely different.

There are several types of chemical reactions, each with unique characteristics. **Synthesis reactions** involve combining elements or simpler compounds to form more complex compounds. For example, hydrogen gas reacts with oxygen gas and forms water. On the flip side, **decomposition reactions** break down compounds into simpler substances. A typical example is the breakdown of hydrogen peroxide into water and oxygen gas.

Combustion reactions are another fascinating type in which substances burn in the presence of oxygen, releasing energy through light and heat. When you light a candle, the wax—a hydrocarbon—reacts with oxygen in the air to produce carbon dioxide, water, and heat. This reaction is why candles burn and provide light. Combustion reactions are also at work when you start your car engine or light a campfire, making them essential to many aspects of daily life, like generating electricity with fossil fuels, as discussed in previous chapters.

Everyday chemical reactions are all around us, often unnoticed. Take the classic baking soda and vinegar reaction, for instance. When you mix these two, they produce carbon dioxide gas, causing fizzing and bubbling. This reaction is fun to watch and demonstrates the principles of chemical change. Another everyday example is the rusting of iron. Iron reacts with oxygen and water and forms iron oxide, commonly known as rust. This slow reaction changes the appearance and strength of the iron, showing how chemical reactions can impact materials over time.

A Chemical Reaction: combustion

Hydrocarbon (e.g. wood) + Oxygen → Carbon Dioxide + Water + Heat and Light (Energy)

For a hands-on activity, try observing the fading of fabric colors in sunlight. Place a piece of colored fabric in direct sunlight and another in the shade. Over a few days, you'll notice the fabric in the sunlight will fade faster. This fading is due to the breaking down of dye molecules by UV light, a chemical reaction accelerated by sunlight. Reflect on how factors like light intensity and exposure time influence the reaction speed and consider practical implications, such as the importance of UV protection for materials and skin.

Another simple activity is observing rust formation on iron nails. Place a few iron nails in a damp environment and watch them develop rust over several days. Reflect on how environmental conditions like humidity and temperature impact the rate of rusting and think about practical applications, such as why protective coatings are crucial for metal structures. If your nails do not rust, check if they have such coatings or are made of special non-rusting alloys.

Chemical reactions are the invisible engines that drive the transformations we see and experience daily. From baking a cake to the rusting of iron, these reactions reveal matter's dynamic and ever-changing nature. Observing and understanding these changes gives us a deeper appreciation for the chemical processes that shape our world.

ACIDS AND BASES: THE SCIENCE OF PH

Imagine biting into a lemon and feeling that sharp, tangy sensation on your tongue. That zing is due to **citric acid**. That is not a band name, although learning about the Citric Acids' music style might be interesting! Anyway, chemically speaking, it is one of many substances known as acids. When dissolved in water, **acids** are compounds that release hydrogen ions. These hydrogen ions give acids their characteristic sour taste and ability to corrode metals. On the flip side, bases are substances that release hydroxide ions in water—a particular molecule comprising parts of hydrogen and oxygen atoms. Bases tend to feel slippery and taste bitter. Think of baking soda or soap—both common bases essential in our daily lives.

To understand how acidic or basic a substance is, we use the so-called pH scale, which ranges from 0 to 14. A pH of 7 is neutral, like pure water. Substances with a pH less than 7 are **acidic**, while those greater than 7 are **basic** (or **alkaline**). For example, lemon juice has a pH of about 2, making it quite acidic. In contrast, baking soda has a pH of about 9, making it mildly basic. This scale helps us measure and understand the chemical properties of different substances, which is crucial in various fields like cooking, medicine, and agriculture.

In our everyday lives, we come across many acids and bases without even realizing it. For example, **vinegar**, often used in salad dressings, is an acid with a pH of around 2–3. It's not only great for adding flavor but also for cleaning due to its acidity. On the other hand, **soap** is a base, which makes it perfect for breaking down oils and grease, helping us stay clean. Another common base is, as mentioned, baking soda, which is used in baking to help the dough rise and is also great for neutralizing odors around the house.

pH plays a significant role in cooking, influencing food's flavor, texture, and color. For instance, the tangy tastes of yogurt and sourdough bread come from lactic acid produced during fermentation. Acids like lemon juice or vinegar can also be used to tenderize meat in marinades by breaking down proteins. In baking, the pH of your ingredients can determine how well your dough rises and the final texture of your baked goods. Understanding pH can help you master these culinary processes!

The importance of pH goes beyond just flavor and cleaning. Maintaining a stable pH is vital for the health of the human body. Our blood, for example, has a pH of around 7.4, slightly basic. This narrow range is essential for properly functioning enzymes and metabolic processes. If the pH of our blood were to shift significantly, it could lead to serious health issues. Our bodies have several mechanisms, like breathing and kidney function, to maintain this delicate balance.

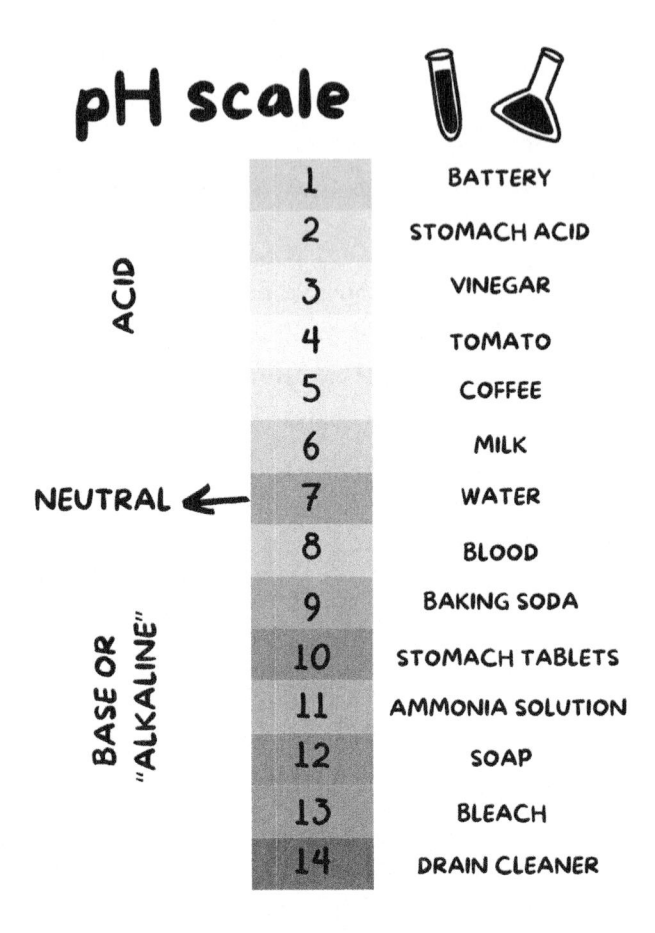

pH scale

pH	
1	BATTERY
2	STOMACH ACID
3	VINEGAR
4	TOMATO
5	COFFEE
6	MILK
7	WATER (NEUTRAL)
8	BLOOD
9	BAKING SODA
10	STOMACH TABLETS
11	AMMONIA SOLUTION
12	SOAP
13	BLEACH
14	DRAIN CLEANER

1–6: ACID
8–14: BASE OR "ALKALINE"

In agriculture, soil pH plays a critical role in plant growth. Different plants thrive at different pH levels. For instance, blueberries prefer acidic soil, while most vegetables grow best in neutral to slightly basic soil. Farmers and gardeners often test soil pH to ensure it suits the crops they want to grow. They might add lime to raise the pH or sulfur to lower it, optimizing the soil conditions for healthy plant growth.

To explore the pH of household products, start by checking the labels of cleaning supplies. Many products will indicate whether they contain acids or bases. Vinegar and lemon-based cleaners are acidic, while ammonia and baking soda are basic. This simple activity can help you understand why certain products are effective at cleaning different types of messes. For example, acidic cleaners are great for removing mineral deposits, while basic cleaners are better for cutting through grease.

Understanding acids, bases, and the pH scale opens a window into the chemical nature of our world. From the food we eat to the products we use, pH plays a vital role in our daily lives. Understanding these scientific facts deepens your appreciation for the invisible chemical science that shapes our experiences.

POLYMERS: THE SCIENCE OF PLASTICS

Have you ever wondered what makes plastic so versatile and ubiquitous in our daily lives? The answer lies in **polymers**, the remarkable materials that form the backbone of many everyday items. Polymers are **long chains of molecules** made up of repeating units called **monomers**. Think of monomers as individual beads on a necklace. When you string them together, you get a polymer. This process of linking monomers to form polymers is known as **polymerization**. Imagine a single paperclip; now, picture a chain of thousands of paperclips linked together. That's what a polymer is—a long, flexible chain of repeating units. The most common elements in these polymers are carbon, hydrogen, oxygen, nitrogen, and some others.

We can divide polymers into two types: natural and synthetic. **Natural polymers** are found in nature and include substances like cellulose and proteins. Cellulose, for example, is the primary component of plant cell walls and gives plants their rigidity.

Proteins, on the other hand, are essential for life, making up everything from your muscles to your hair. We touched on proteins as one of the main macronutrients in the chapter around the human body. However, **synthetic polymers**, also commonly known as **plastics**, are manufactured and include materials like polyethylene and nylon. Plastic bags and bottles are made of polyethylene, while nylon is used in fabrics and fishing lines. These synthetic polymers —typically made of crude oil—are created through chemical processes that mimic the natural polymerization found in nature.

Polymers have become incredibly important in our daily lives. They're used to make a wide variety of products, from plastic water bottles and food containers to clothing fibers and automotive parts. Polymers' versatility comes from their ability to be molded into different shapes and forms while being robust and light, making them ideal for countless applications. For instance, the plastic bottle many of us drink from is made from polyethylene terephthalate, PET, a durable and lightweight polymer.

Your favorite fleece jacket might be made from polyester, another artificial polymer that provides warmth and comfort. Even the tires on your car are made from rubber, which can be made from natural or artificial polymers that offer the perfect combination of flexibility and strength.

However, the widespread use of polymers, particularly plastics, has a significant environmental impact. Plastic pollution is a growing concern, as discarded plastics can take hundreds of years to decompose. They accumulate in landfills, rivers, and oceans, threatening wildlife and ecosystems. Recycling efforts are crucial in mitigating this issue, but not all plastics are easily recyclable. Understanding the environmental impact of polymers encourages us to make more sustainable choices, like using reusable bags and bottles and supporting recycling programs.

CHEMISTRY AROUND US 133

Plastic Types and their Recycling Difficulties

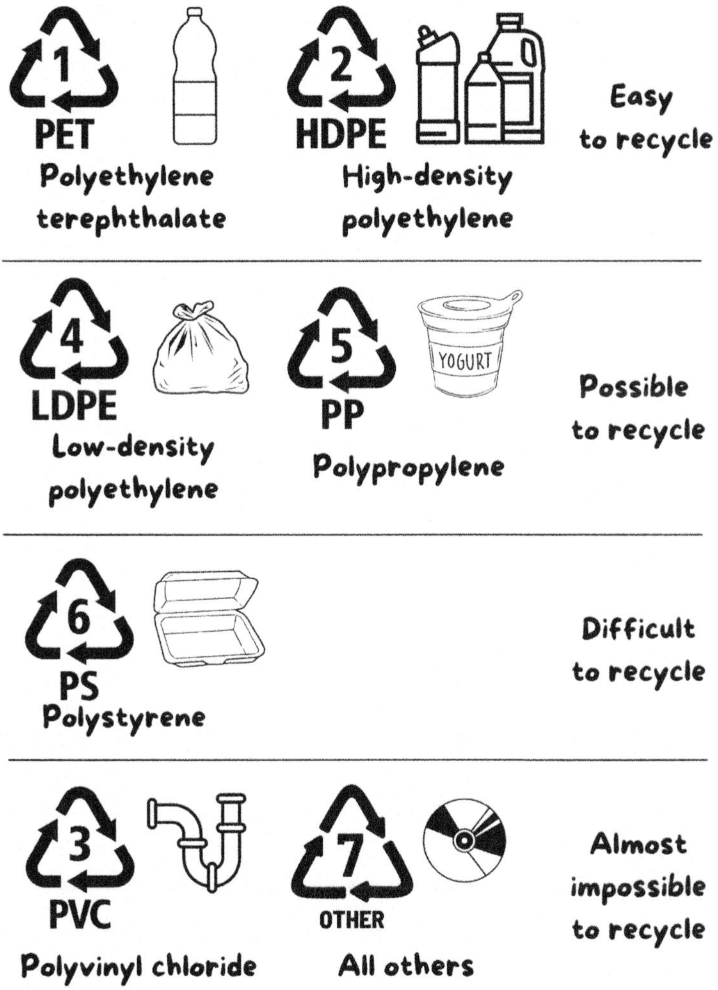

1 PET — Polyethylene terephthalate

2 HDPE — High-density polyethylene

Easy to recycle

4 LDPE — Low-density polyethylene

5 PP — Polypropylene

Possible to recycle

6 PS — Polystyrene

Difficult to recycle

3 PVC — Polyvinyl chloride

7 OTHER — All others

Almost impossible to recycle

To explore the world of polymers firsthand, consider observing plastic degradation in the environment. Walk around your neighborhood or a local park and look for plastic items in different conditions. You might find plastic bags caught in trees, plastic bottles on the ground, or plastic playground equipment exposed to the elements. Observe how these items change over time. Do they become brittle and discolored? Do they break down into smaller pieces? Reflect on how weather conditions like sunlight, rain, and temperature affect the degradation rate. This activity highlights the durability of plastics and reminds us about the importance of proper disposal and recycling. In any case, all of us are invited to dispose of plastics properly if we see them in places where they do not belong.

Polymers are fascinating and multifaceted materials vital to modern life. They are everywhere, from the clothes to the gadgets we wear. While they offer numerous benefits, their environmental impact reminds us of the need for responsible usage and disposal. By exploring and understanding polymers, we can appreciate their contributions to our world and take steps toward a more sustainable future.

THE CHEMISTRY OF COOKING: HOW HEAT TRANSFORMS FOOD

Imagine you're in the kitchen, stirring a pot as water boils on the stove and steam rises into the air. What you're witnessing is more than just cooking—it's a live chemistry lesson! Heat is at work here, changing the water from one form to another. First, if you had ice, it would melt into liquid water, and with more heat, that water would turn into steam, which is gas. These changes happen because heat makes the water molecules move faster and spread apart.

This basic idea in chemistry explains everything from why your **solid** ice cubes melt to become **liquid** in a glass to how water eventually evaporates, reaching a **gas**eous state. Heat is like a magic wand in the kitchen, transforming ingredients and making your favorite dishes possible!

Now, consider how different foods respond to heat. Take butter, for instance. When you melt butter in a pan, heat causes it to transition from a solid to a liquid. The molecules gain energy and move more freely, changing the butter's physical state. Similarly, heat causes the proteins inside an egg to denature when you boil the egg. This means the proteins unfold and form new bonds, changing from a runny liquid to a firm solid.

We have witnessed one of the fundamental principles in the science of chemistry: the **three states of matter**—solid, liquid, and gas. We have also observed one possibility for how matter can change from one state to another: **heat**. We could also express it as **temperature**, as cooling down would also work—just the other way around when we make ice out of water. For completeness, extreme pressures can also affect the state of matter.

Heat also transforms textures and flavors, making these processes practical and fascinating to observe. Often enough, they even make foods digestible for humans, and tastier.

One of the most delicious transformations in cooking is the **Maillard Reaction**. This is the scientific process behind the browning of foods, creating those rich, complex flavors we love in toasted bread, grilled meat, and roasted coffee. When heat is applied, sugars and proteins in the food react, forming new compounds that give browned foods their distinctive taste and aroma. Next time you're toasting bread, take a moment to observe how it gets golden, and smell the delicious aroma.

This is the Maillard Reaction in action, turning simple ingredients into culinary delights.

Heat also has a profound effect on proteins and starches. When you fry an egg, the heat causes the egg whites and yolk to solidify. This process, known as **denaturation**, involves the proteins in the egg unfolding and forming new firm structures. Similarly, heat causes the starches to gelatinize when you cook pasta or potatoes. This means the starch granules absorb water and swell, transforming from hard and crunchy to soft and chewy. This is why raw potatoes and pasta are hard, but cooking them makes them tender and delicious.

Emulsification is another fascinating concept in cooking, where heat helps mix liquids that don't usually blend or respectively mix with each other easily, like oil and water. This process creates stable mixtures called emulsions, which are essential in making mayonnaise, salad dressings, and even hollandaise sauce. When you whisk oil into vinegar or lemon juice, adding a bit of heat can help the mixture combine smoothly. For example, when making a vinaigrette, you might notice that the oil and vinegar blend better as you whisk vigorously. This is emulsification at work, creating a delicious and stable dressing for your salad.

Cooking combines art and science, where heat transforms ingredients into mouth-watering dishes. Understanding these chemical processes not only enhances your cooking skills but also deepens your appreciation for the chemistry happening in your kitchen. From boiling water to frying eggs and creating emulsions, heat is the magical element that turns raw ingredients into culinary masterpieces. So next time you're in the kitchen, remember the science behind the sizzle and enjoy the delicious results.

Chemistry is everywhere, even in the meals we prepare and enjoy. The transformations driven by heat, the reactions that create flavors, and the delicate balance of emulsions all highlight the intricate dance of molecules. As we wrap up our exploration of chemistry, let's turn our attention to the wonders of Earth science and geology, where we'll uncover the secrets of our planet's structure and the forces that shape it.

CHAPTER SEVEN
EARTH SCIENCE AND GEOLOGY UNCOVERED

Have you ever wondered what forces shape the Earth beneath our feet? Earth's surface constantly changes from fiery volcanoes erupting with molten rock to glaciers slowly carving out valleys. In this chapter, we'll explore the powerful natural events that mold our planet, like **Volcanoes**, where mountains of fire rise from deep within, and **Earthquakes**, when the ground suddenly shakes and shifts. We'll also uncover the secrets of the **Rock Cycle**, which transforms rocks over millions of years, discover how **Glaciers**, nature's ice sculptors, slowly reshape landscapes, remember **Fossils**, the ancient clues that reveal Earth's distant past, and the **Water Cycle**, which keeps water moving from rain to rivers, powering life across the planet. Let's dive into the exciting world of **Earth Science and Geology**, where every rock, wave, and tremor tells a story!

VOLCANOES: EARTH'S FIERY MOUNTAINS

Volcanoes are one of nature's most awe-inspiring phenomena. At their core, volcanoes are openings in the Earth's crust that allow **molten rock**, ash, and gases to escape from below the surface.

This molten rock originates in a **magma** chamber, a vast reservoir of molten rock stored beneath the Earth's crust. When pressure builds up in the magma chamber, it forces the magma to move upward through a vent, an opening that leads to the surface. As the magma reaches the surface, it erupts, releasing magma—now called **lava**—, ash, and gases. The crater, a bowl-shaped depression at the volcano's summit, forms due to these explosive events.

There are several types of volcanoes, each with unique characteristics and eruption styles. **Shield volcanoes**, like Mauna Loa in Hawaii, are characterized by their broad, gently sloping sides. Built almost entirely from fluid lava flows, these volcanoes can cover extensive areas. Mauna Loa is the world's largest active shield volcano, and its eruptions are typically less violent, with lava flowing steadily from fissures and vents.

In contrast, **stratovolcanoes**, or **composite volcanoes**, are steep sided and known for their explosive eruptions. Mount St. Helens in Washington State is a prime example. These volcanoes are built from alternating layers of lava flows, ash, and volcanic rocks. When they erupt, they can produce powerful explosions that send ash clouds high into the atmosphere and pyroclastic flows—deadly, fast-moving currents of hot gas and volcanic matter—down their slopes.

Cinder cone volcanoes are smaller and more conical in shape. Parícutin in Mexico is one of them. These volcanoes are formed from volcanic fragments called cinders ejected from a single vent. Over time, the cinders accumulate around the vent, creating a circular or oval cone with a bowl-shaped crater at the top. Parícutin is particularly notable because it emerged suddenly in a farmer's cornfield in 1943 and continued to erupt for nine years, growing to over 1,200 feet in height.

SHIELD VOLCANO   **COMPOSITE VOLCANO**   **CINDER CONE VOLCANO**

Volcanic eruptions can have significant impacts on the environment and human life. Lava flows, streams of hot molten rock reaching temperatures of more than 700°C or 1,300°F, respectively, can destroy everything in their path, including homes, roads, and forests. While lava flows move relatively slowly, allowing people to evacuate, they cause severe damage to infrastructure and landscapes. Ash clouds, composed of tiny volcanic particles, can affect air travel, as ash can clog airplane engines and reduce visibility. Additionally, ash can pose respiratory health risks, particularly for individuals with preexisting conditions.

One of the most dangerous aspects of volcanic eruptions is pyroclastic flows. These are fast-moving avalanches of hot gas, ash, and volcanic rocks that can travel down the slopes of a volcano at speeds of up to 700 kilometers or 430 miles per hour. They obliterate everything in their path, making them incredibly deadly. The eruption of Mount Vesuvius in 79 CE, about 2000 years ago, which buried the Roman cities of Pompeii and Herculaneum, located in today's Italy, is a stark reminder of the destructive power of pyroclastic flows. The towns were engulfed in ash and volcanic debris, preserving them for centuries. Today, the well-conserved remains can be visited and are located near Naples, Italy, in Europe.

To stay safe during volcanic eruptions, it's crucial to have evacuation plans and emergency kits ready. Authorities typically provide warnings to the communities affected and evacuation orders when a volcano shows signs of imminent eruption. Following these instructions can save lives. It's also wise to have an emergency kit containing essentials like food, water, masks, and first-aid supplies.

But volcanoes are also a source of great beauty. You can find a group of stunning islands in the Pacific, where crystal-clear waters reveal vibrant coral reefs teeming with life. These islands, such as the ones in Hawaii and the Solomon Islands, are tropical paradises today and have a fiery history! Beneath the beauty of the ocean, these islands are actually the peaks of ancient volcanoes that erupted long ago. Over time, the tops of these volcanic mountains rose above the surface, while coral reefs began to grow and thrive around their submerged bases. Today, these reefs are home to countless fish, coral, and marine life species, turning the remnants of volcanic activity into underwater wonders!

Understanding volcanoes helps us appreciate the dynamic nature of our planet and the forces that shape its surface. From the gentle lava flows of shield volcanoes to the explosive eruptions of stratovolcanoes, these fiery mountains remind us of the powerful geological processes beneath our feet. So, the next time you see a volcanic landscape, take a moment to marvel at the incredible forces that created it.

EARTHQUAKES: WHEN THE GROUND SHAKES

Have you ever felt the ground tremble beneath your feet and wondered what causes such an unsettling experience? Earthquakes result from the shifting and breaking of Earth's **tectonic plates**. Picture the Earth's crust as a giant jigsaw puzzle of several large and small pieces called tectonic plates. These plates are constantly moving, albeit very slowly, due to the convective currents in the semi-fluid mantle beneath them. In other words, the Earth's tectonic plates move because the hot, molten rock beneath them, called magma, constantly shifts. As the magma heats up, it sometimes erupts, as discussed in the last section. However, it usually rises and then cools, creating a slow-moving current that pushes the plates around like rafts on a river. This process is called **convection**, which causes continents to drift and mountains to form! When these plates grind against each other at fault lines—fractures in the Earth's crust—they can get stuck due to friction. Over time, stress builds up, and when it gets too much, the plates suddenly slip, releasing a burst of energy in the form of seismic waves. These seismic waves travel through the Earth, causing the ground to shake.

To understand and measure these earth-shaking events, scientists use specialized instruments called **seismographs**. A seismograph records the ground motion caused by seismic waves, producing a graph known as a seismogram. By analyzing seismograms, scientists can determine an earthquake's location, depth, and magnitude. One of the most well-known scales for measuring earthquakes is the **Richter Scale**, which quantifies the energy an earthquake releases. However, the Richter Scale has been largely replaced by the **Moment Magnitude Scale** (Mw) because it accurately represents an earthquake's size, especially for larger quakes.

The Moment Magnitude Scale considers the area of the fault that slipped, the amount of slip, and the rocks' strength.

The effects of earthquakes can be devastating, reshaping landscapes and bringing human structures to the ground. Ground shaking, the most immediate effect, can cause buildings to collapse, bridges to tumble, and roads to buckle. The intensity of ground shaking depends on factors like the earthquake's magnitude, the distance from the **epicenter**—the actual center of the quake—and the type of ground materials. Soft soils and sediments can amplify shaking, leading to more severe damage. Surface rupture is another dramatic effect, where the ground physically breaks and shifts along the fault line, creating visible cracks and displacement of the Earth's surface. This can disrupt infrastructure, severing roads and pipelines and even splitting buildings.

The secondary effects of earthquakes can be equally catastrophic. **Tsunamis**, colossal ocean waves triggered by underwater earthquakes, can inundate coastal areas, causing widespread destruction and loss of life. The 2011 Tōhoku earthquake in the Western Pacific East of Japan, which had a magnitude of 9.0, generated a massive sea wave, which is then called a tsunami, that devastated coastal communities and led to the Fukushima nuclear disaster. Landslides, triggered by the shaking, can bury villages and block rivers, leading to flooding. Fires are another common secondary effect, often ignited by ruptured gas lines and downed power lines. The Great San Francisco Earthquake of 1906, which had an estimated magnitude of 7.9, is primarily remembered for the fires that raged through the city, causing more destruction than the quake itself.

Being prepared for an earthquake is crucial for safety. The "Drop, Cover, and Hold On" drill is one of the most effective safety measures. When you feel the ground shaking, immediately drop to your hands and knees to prevent being knocked over, cover your head and neck with your arms, take shelter under a sturdy piece of furniture, and hold on until the shaking stops. It's also important to have an emergency kit containing essentials like water, food, a flashlight, a first-aid kit, and any necessary medications. Familiarize yourself with the evacuation routes and emergency plans in your area.

Understanding the causes and outcomes of earthquakes and taking proactive safety measures can help mitigate the impact of these natural disasters. By staying informed and prepared, you can navigate the challenges of the Earth's restless crust.

THE ROCK CYCLE: HOW ROCKS TRANSFORM

Likely, you've picked up many rocks while outside. Maybe you were wondering about their journey through time. The rock cycle is the continuous process of transformation that rocks undergo, changing from one type to another through various geological processes. Let's start with **igneous rocks**, which form from cooled magma or lava, which is why scientists have also designated them **magnetites**. When molten rock cools and solidifies beneath the Earth's surface, it becomes igneous rock. If this happens underground, the rock is called **intrusive** or **plutonic**, like **granite** found in Yosemite National Park, known for its large, visible crystals. However, suppose the cooling occurs on the surface after a volcanic eruption. In that case, the rock is **extrusive** or **volcanic**, such as basalt.

Over time, weathering and erosion break down these igneous rocks into smaller particles called **sediments**. Weathering is when wind, water, and temperature changes result in chemical alterations and the physical breakdowns of the rocks at the Earth's surface. **Erosion**, on the other hand, is the process of transporting these sediments by natural forces like rivers, wind, or glaciers. When these sediments accumulate in layers and are buried over long periods, they undergo compaction and cementation, forming sedimentary rocks. An excellent example of a sedimentary rock is **sandstone**, which you can see in the majestic formations of the Grand Canyon. Sandstone forms from compacted sand grains, often displaying beautiful layers that tell the story of ancient environments.

But the rock cycle continues. When sedimentary rocks are buried deep within the Earth, they are subjected to intense heat and pressure, transforming them into **metamorphic rocks**. This process, known as metamorphism, alters the mineral composition and structure of the rocks without melting them. For instance, this process can transform **limestone**, a sedimentary rock, into **marble**, a metamorphic rock.

Marble is prized for its beauty and strength, making it popular for sculptures and buildings. Famous examples are the iconic sculptures of ancient Greece and Rome or the marble used for antique Chinese vases. Marble is not to be mixed with **ceramics**, which are clay-based, synthetic, and artificial substances and typically less durable.

The cycle continues as these metamorphic rocks might be pushed deeper into the Earth, where they may melt again, forming magma. When this magma eventually cools, it forms new igneous rocks, and the cycle starts anew. This endless transformation illustrates the dynamic nature of our planet, constantly reshaping the rocks that make up the Earth's crust.

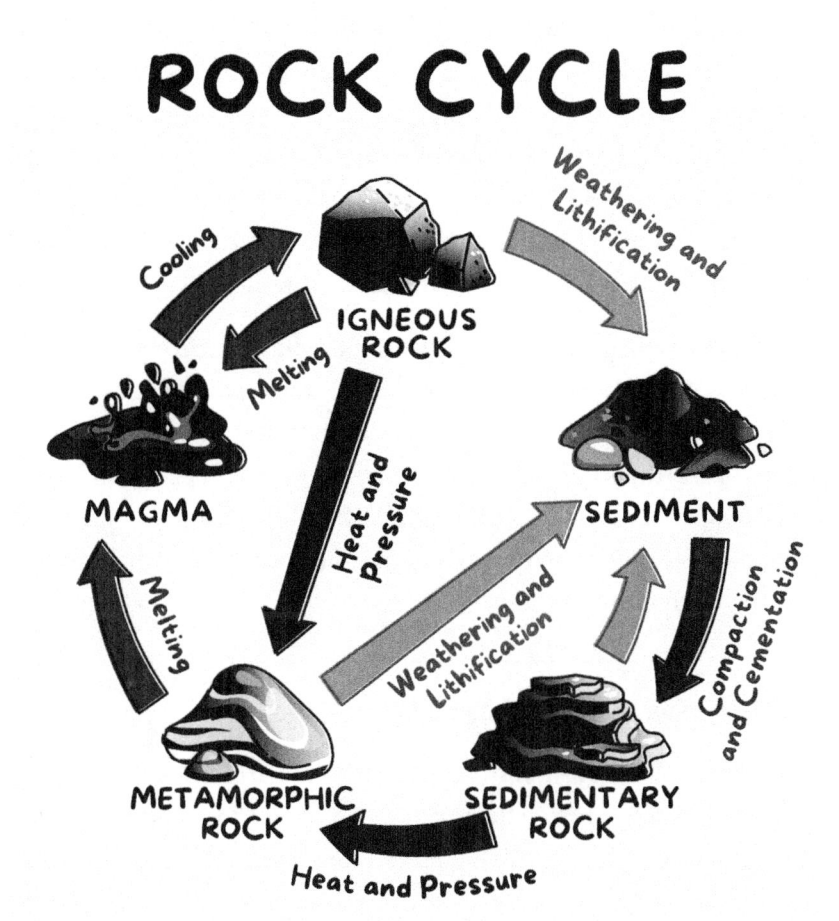

ROCK CYCLE

Cooling · *Weathering and Lithification*

IGNEOUS ROCK

Melting

MAGMA

Heat and Pressure

Melting

Weathering and Lithification

SEDIMENT

Compaction and Cementation

METAMORPHIC ROCK

SEDIMENTARY ROCK

Heat and Pressure

To better understand the rock cycle, an engaging activity you can do is rock identification using local samples. Start by collecting rocks from different areas, such as a riverbed, a park, or your backyard. Examine each rock closely, looking for visual properties to help you identify its type. Igneous rocks often have a crystalline texture with visible mineral grains. Sedimentary rocks might display layers or contain fossils, and metamorphic rocks usually have a foliated or banded appearance. For example, if you find a rock with distinct layers, it's likely sedimentary. If it has a glassy or fine-grained texture, it could be igneous.

Creating a rock cycle diagram can also be a helpful visual aid. Draw and label each type of rock—igneous, sedimentary, and metamorphic—along with the processes that transform them: melting and cooling, weathering and erosion, compaction and cementation, and heat and pressure. This visual representation can help you see the connections between the different types of rocks and the processes that drive their transformations.

Understanding the rock cycle gives you insight into the natural processes that shape our planet. Each rock you encounter has undergone a remarkable journey, bearing witness to the dynamic forces of Earth. So, the next time you pick up a rock, think about its possible history and the incredible transformations it has experienced. Volcanic activity, earthquakes, or weather likely brought it there—maybe all of them.

GLACIERS: EARTH'S ICE SCULPTORS

A massive, giant, slow-moving river of ice stretches for miles—this is a glacier, a powerful force to be found in nature. Glaciers are formed over thousands of years from layers of snow piling up and getting compressed under their own weight. Each winter, new snow falls, and over time, the weight of the layers squeezes the snow underneath into solid ice. But glaciers aren't just frozen in place; they move! As more snow and ice build up, gravity causes the glacier to slide slowly, dragging along rocks and debris with it. As glaciers advance and retreat, they act like massive bulldozers, carving valleys, shaping mountains, and leaving behind new landscapes in their wake. Their movements are controlled by temperature, snowfall, and pressure, making glaciers both sculptors of the Earth and incredible records of our planet's history.

The life cycle of a glacier is fascinating. These ice giants grow during periods of cold climate when snowfall is abundant and temperatures are low enough to prevent significant melting. Conversely, they shrink during warmer periods when melting outpaces snowfall. Glaciers are crucial for Earth's freshwater storage, holding more than 60% of the world's fresh water. They release this water slowly into rivers and lakes, providing a steady supply even during dry seasons. However, warmer phases in recent times have been causing glacier melting, which, if continued, threatens this vital water source and contributes to rising sea levels.

Glaciers are nature's sculptors, carving out stunning landscapes as they move. As glaciers advance, they erode the land beneath them, gouging out valleys and fjords. When they retreat, they leave behind unique landforms such as U-shaped valleys, hanging valleys, and moraine, which are accumulations of dirt and rocks. The Yosemite Valley in California is a prime example of glacial carving, with its deep, U-shaped valley and sheer granite cliffs. The fjords of Norway, with their steep, glacially carved cliffs and deep waters, offer another breathtaking example. These landscapes are not only beautiful but also provide valuable insights into the geological history of the regions.

Different types of glaciers add to the diversity of these icy wonders. **Valley glaciers** form in high mountain valleys, flowing down like rivers of ice. As they move, they carve out deep valleys and rugged landscapes. The Franz Josef Glacier in New Zealand is a remarkable example, descending from the Southern Alps into a temperate rainforest, creating a unique and dynamic environment. **Ice sheets** and **ice caps** are massive glaciers covering vast areas, such as in Greenland and Antarctica. These ice masses play a crucial role in regulating global sea levels. The Lambert Glacier in Antarctica is the world's largest glacier, stretching over 400 kilometers or 250 miles and contributing significantly to the Antarctic ice sheet.

Piedmont glaciers spread out at the base of mountains, forming broad, fan-shaped ice fields. The Malaspina Glacier in Alaska is a stunning example, where the ice flows from the St. Elias Mountains and spreads out over the coastal plain. **Tidewater glaciers**, on the other hand, flow directly into the ocean, where chunks of ice break off and form icebergs. The Columbia Glacier in

Alaska is a notable tidewater glacier known for its rapid retreat and the large icebergs it calves into Prince William Sound.

Famous glaciers worldwide capture the imagination with their sheer size and beauty. The Perito Moreno Glacier in Argentina is renowned for its dramatic icefalls and accessibility to visitors. Unlike many glaciers, Perito Moreno is stable, neither advancing nor retreating significantly, making it a popular tourist destination. The Franz Josef Glacier, as mentioned earlier, offers a rare opportunity to see a glacier amidst lush rainforest. The Lambert Glacier, with its immense size, underscores the scale and power of Antarctic ice masses.

Drilling into glaciers also allows scientists to explore layers of ice that have remained frozen for centuries, preserving tiny bubbles of ancient air, dust, and even microorganisms. Each layer acts like a time capsule, revealing geological information about past climates, volcanic eruptions, and biological clues, such as ancient pollen or bacteria, offering a glimpse into the Earth's ecosystems from long ago. These frozen layers help us understand how the planet's environment and life forms have changed.

Glaciers show sensitivity to temperature variations, making them valuable markers for scientists studying the influence of prolonged warm periods. In recent decades, glaciers worldwide have been retreating. As glaciers melt over prolonged periods, they contribute to sea level rise, which can lead to the displacement of coastal communities and changes in weather patterns. Efforts to monitor and preserve glaciers include satellite tracking and scientific expeditions, providing critical data to understand and mitigate the impacts of such prolonged melting phases.

Intriguing phenomena associated with glaciers add to their mystique. Glacial blue ice, for instance, appears vibrant blue because of the way ice crystals absorb and scatter light. The longer the path length of the light within the ice, the bluer it appears. Glacier mice are another curious phenomenon—small, moss-covered rocks that move across glacier surfaces. These rocks, found in places like Iceland, seem to move in unison, though the exact mechanism behind their movement remains a mystery. Some glaciers also produce eerie, thunderous sounds as they move and crack. These sounds, known as icequakes, result from the glacier's internal stresses and the movement of ice over bedrock.

FOSSILS: CLUES TO EARTH'S PAST

Imagine you took the hint from the rock cycle section earlier in this section and stumbled upon a rock with a mysterious imprint —a leaf, a shell, or perhaps a bone. You've found a fossil, a preserved remnant of ancient life. Fossils form through a process called **fossilization**, where the remains of plants, animals, or other organisms are preserved in sedimentary rock. When an organism dies, it often gets buried under layers of sediment. Over time, these layers harden into rock, and the organic material may slowly be replaced by minerals, creating a stone replica of the original organism. There are two main types of fossils: **body fossils**, which are the actual remains of the organism, like bones or shells, and **trace fossils**, which are evidence of the organism's activities, such as footprints or burrows. Fossils provide invaluable insights into past environments, helping us understand the organisms that once roamed the Earth and their living conditions.

Unearthing these ancient treasures requires meticulous work by paleontologists and scientists who study fossils. The process begins with **excavation**, where paleontologists carefully dig out fossils from rock layers. This work often involves using small tools like brushes and chisels to avoid damaging the delicate remains. Once excavated, the fossils are usually encased in plaster jackets for safe transport to laboratories. Dating these fossils is crucial for placing them in the correct period. **Relative dating** involves examining the layers of rock in which the fossil was found. In contrast, **radiometric dating** uses the decay of radioactive isotopes to determine the fossil's age more precisely. After dating, paleontologists reconstruct the fossils, piecing together fragmented remains like a complex puzzle. This reconstruction helps scientists visualize the organism and understand its anatomy and behavior. Yet again, paleontologists have to have a certain insight and knowledge into geology, biology, and chemistry to properly judge what they discover. This shows how many science fields need to play together to uncover the secrets of our world.

Some fossil discoveries have profoundly impacted our understanding of life's history. One famous discovery is Archaeopteryx, which was found in Germany in 1861. Its name is derived from Greek and can be translated as "ancient wing." This fossil showed a crucial link between dinosaurs and birds, with features of both groups, such as feathers and a bony tail. Such discoveries have reshaped our knowledge of biological history, highlighting the connections between different species. Another fascinating fossil discovery was that of the Ichthyosaur, found by **Mary Anning** in the early 1800s along the cliffs of England. This fossil was of a massive marine reptile that lived during the time of the dinosaurs, resembling a cross between a fish and a dolphin. The Ichthyosaur discovery was crucial because it provided the first solid evidence that reptiles once ruled the seas, just as dinosaurs did on land. This fossil helped scientists understand life in ancient oceans. It revealed how some species adapted to live in water millions of years ago. Anning's findings paved the way for future discoveries in paleontology, showing how much life on Earth has changed over time.

Fossil hunting can be an exciting and educational activity. On your next hike (yes, another one!), combine your adventure with a fossil exploration. Rivers and valleys are often great places to find fossils because water can expose sedimentary rock layers. Look for areas with exposed rock formations, and watch for imprints or unusual shapes. Rocks near rivers can contain fossils, especially if the area was once underwater. Remember to bring a small brush and a magnifying glass to examine your finds more closely. When you find a potential fossil, take a moment to reflect on its history. Think about the ancient world it came from and the processes that preserved it through millions of years.

Fossils are more than just remnants of the past; they are windows into Earth's history, offering clues about the life that once thrived on our planet. Each fossil tells a story, from the creature's life to its eventual preservation in rock. By piecing all the findings together, we gain a deeper appreciation for the complex history of life on Earth. So, next time you're out and about, keep your eyes peeled for these ancient treasures—you never know what you might discover.

THE WATER CYCLE: FROM RAIN TO RIVERS

Imagine you're a tiny water droplet drifting lazily in a backyard pond. But your journey didn't start here; it certainly doesn't end here! You're part of the Earth's incredible water cycle—a never-ending adventure. A typical journey of yours begins as the Sun's warmth gently lifts you into the air, transforming you into **vapor** during evaporation. Up you float, higher and higher, joining millions of other droplets in the sky. As you rise, you feel the air around you getting cooler, causing you and your fellow droplets to huddle together and form fluffy **clouds**.

Before long, the clouds grow heavy, and it's time for you to return to Earth. Depending on the temperature, you might fall as **rain**, **snow**, or even **hail**, landing on a mountain, a tree, or maybe back into that same pond. But your journey doesn't stop there! If you land on a leaf, a plant might absorb and release you again through transpiration, sending you back into the air. Or, you might soak into the ground, seeping deep into the Earth to refill underground reservoirs, join a river on its way to the ocean, or even become part of a **photosynthetic reaction** of a plant, helping it grow and providing oxygen to our atmosphere! You remember?

Wherever you go, you're part of a constant cycle, moving, changing, and helping to sustain life on Earth!

Each stage of the water cycle plays a crucial role in maintaining Earth's environmental balance. **Transpiration**, for example, is vital for plants as it helps them absorb nutrients from the soil and cools them through evaporation. **Infiltration** replenishes groundwater supplies essential for drinking water, agriculture, and maintaining natural habitats. **Runoff**, meanwhile, carries nutrients and sediments that enrich soils and support aquatic ecosystems. This interconnected system supports life by distributing water where it's needed most, from plants' roots to the oceans' depths.

The water cycle also significantly influences **weather** patterns and climate. The movement of water vapor and its condensation into clouds play a crucial role in forming weather systems. For instance, ocean evaporation drives the formation of tropical storms and hurricanes. These powerful weather events can significantly impact coastal regions, bringing heavy rain, strong winds, and flooding. On a broader scale, the distribution of precipitation shapes climate zones, affecting everything from desert landscapes to lush rainforests. This versatility is why we see water as ice in glaciers, liquid in oceans, and vapor in the atmosphere.

Water is a marvel in itself. Did you know that about 71% of the Earth's surface is covered by water, yet only about 2.5% is fresh? As we found out in the earlier chapter, a significant portion of that fresh water is locked away in glaciers and ice caps. This scarcity makes the water cycle even more critical for sustaining life. Water is also unique in its ability to exist in all three states—solid, liquid, and gas—within the natural temperature range found on Earth. Yet again, it is remarkable that the Earth is in the exact right spot from the Sun to get the right light and temperature. Remember the cosmic shielding from its own unique magnetic field and the giant planets in the outer solar system.

Understanding the water cycle helps us appreciate the vital processes that sustain life and shape our world. From the evaporation of water into the sky to its return to the ground as precipitation, each step is a testament to the delicate balance of nature. So, the next time you see rain falling or a river flowing, remember the incredible journey water has taken to get there. With this knowledge, we can better appreciate the importance of conserving and protecting our precious water resources.

Earth science and geology reveal the dynamic processes that have shaped our planet for ages. From the fiery eruptions of volcanoes to the relentless grinding of glaciers, these forces have sculpted the landscapes we see today.

CONCLUSION

And here we are, at the end of our scientific adventure! We've journeyed through the vast expanse of space, delved into the wonders of life, and explored the incredible mechanics of the human body. We've dissected the principles of physics and engineering that govern our everyday lives and unraveled the complex world of chemistry. Earth sciences concluded our journey. If you've ever wondered how the world around you works, I hope this book has provided some satisfying answers.

Throughout our journey, we've tackled some big questions. We started by exploring the marvels of robotics and engineering. From the basics of how robots work to the intricacies of bridge engineering and the science of flight, we've seen how human ingenuity can create amazing machines and structures. We've also looked at the future of renewable energy and learned from past engineering failures.

In biology, we've uncovered animal superpowers and communication science among creatures. We've marveled at bioluminescent wonders and the photosynthetic magic of plants. The world of microorganisms and the blueprint of life, DNA, have shown us that even the smallest entities play crucial roles in our lives.

Astronomy took us on a cosmic journey through our solar system, the life cycle of stars, and the mysteries of black holes. We've also explored the Milky Way, our home galaxy, and speculated about planets beyond our solar system. The wonders of the universe are limitless and endlessly fascinating.

When we focused on the human body, we explored the brain's incredible capabilities, the circulatory system's vital role, and the digestive system's complex processes. We've also delved into the immune system's defense mechanisms, the skeletal system's support structure, and the importance of sleep.

Physics has shown us the fundamental forces at play in our daily lives. Gravity keeps us grounded; simple machines make our work easier, and magnetism and electricity power our world. Sound and light have revealed the wonders of our auditory and visual experiences.

Chemistry has explained the building blocks of matter, the periodic table's magic, and chemical reactions' transformative power. We've also explored the science of acids, bases, and polymers and seen how heat transforms food in the kitchen.

Finally, Earth science and geology have brought us closer to the dynamic processes that shape our planet. From the fiery eruptions of volcanoes to the relentless grinding of glaciers, we've seen how these forces sculpt the landscapes we know today. We've also uncovered the secrets of fossils and the continuous movement of water through the water cycle.

What are our Key Takeaways? Just try to remember that:

1. **Curiosity Fuels Discovery**: Never stop asking questions. The world is full of wonders waiting to be explored.
2. **Science is Everywhere**: From the smallest microorganism to the vastness of space, science explains the world around us.
3. **Learning is a Lifelong Journey**: Science is constantly evolving. Stay curious and keep learning.

Now, it's your turn. Whether you're a student, a parent, or someone who loves to learn, take what you've discovered and explore further. The sweep over these different fields is also about finding out where a curiosity spark is. In my case, it was Mechanical Engineering. Is yours Chemistry or even Biochemistry? The profession of a scientist or engineer is deeply fulfilling. If you've experienced such a spark hitting you, I'd be one of the happiest authors around!

Conduct your experiments, observe the natural world, and discuss findings with your family and friends. Share the excitement of discovery and inspire others to be curious about the world around them. And, of course, if you are considering going into science as a professional—that would be a win-win!

As a father and someone who has spent a lifetime immersed in science and technology, I've experienced that the joy of discovery is one of the greatest gifts you can give yourself. Science is not just about memorizing hundreds of details; it's about understanding how things work, why they happen, and what they mean for our lives.

Remember, scientists are always on a journey, and gaining knowledge is not a destination. Keep your curiosity alive, and you'll find that the world is an endless source of wonder and excitement. Thank you for joining me on this adventure.

I look forward to it, having sparked a lifelong love of learning and a deeper appreciation for our incredible world.

Stay curious, keep exploring, and most importantly, have fun with science!

I will leave you with a quote from Albert Einstein, one of the 20th-century's most famous scientists:

> *"I have no special talents. I am only passionately curious."*

Warmest regards, Martin Villoria

Share the Facts and Spread the Learning Fun

There is no doubt that education is essential for young minds and it's hard to see any child not enjoying every aspect of their lives. As the children in your life continue to be entertained with relevant and practical information, remember that you can help others do the same.

LEAVE A REVIEW!

I hope you have thoroughly enjoyed not just learning about such a wide range of topics but also sharing them with others. I ask for one last share so that others can hear your opinions because they are more important than you can imagine. Thank you so much and I can't wait to hear from you.

Scan the QR code below

BONUS CHAPTER: FAMILY QUIZ & FUN FACTS

Welcome to the bonus family quiz chapter! This section is an interactive, fun, and educational way for families to engage with the science concepts covered in the book. The first two sub-chapters provide several quiz-type questions around the book's content, first as multiple-choice and then a collection of true or false ones. The third and last chapter closes with a random collection of fun fact tidbits. Whether you're on vacation, like on a road trip, or you'd like to convince your family to take the phones away or turn off all devices, try it and enjoy.

MULTIPLE-CHOICE QUESTIONS

This quiz provides multiple-choice questions across all fields discussed in this book.

1. What is the main function of a robot's sensors?

   a) To power the robot
   b) To detect the environment
   c) To move the robot's parts
   d) To store energy

2. Who is known as the father of the computer?

   a) Alan Turing
   b) Charles Babbage
   c) Bill Gates

d) Steve Jobsa

3. Which type of bridge uses a combination of cables and towers to support the bridge deck?

a) Beam bridge
b) Arch bridge
c) Suspension bridge
d) Truss bridge

4. What pigment gives plants their green color and plays a crucial role in photosynthesis?

a) Hemoglobin
b) Melanin
c) Chlorophyll
d) Keratin

5. How do dolphins communicate with each other using sound?

a) Echolocation
b) Electromagnetism
c) Bioluminescence
d) Infrared signals

6. Which process describes a caterpillar transforming into a butterfly?

a) Photosynthesis
b) Metamorphosis
c) Respiration
d) Fermentation

7. Which planet is known as the "Red Planet"?

   a) Mercury
   b) Venus
   c) Mars
   d) Jupiter

8. What is the main component of a star's early stage, also known as a protostar?

   a) Dust and gas
   b) Solid rock
   c) Water and ice
   d) Metal and minerals

9. What is a black hole's event horizon?

   a) The point where light cannot escape
   b) The center of the black hole
   c) The outer atmosphere of a black hole
   d) The region where stars form

10. What part of the brain controls balance and coordination?

    a) Cerebrum
    b) Cerebellum
    c) Brainstem
    d) Hippocampus

11. Which component of blood is responsible for clotting?

    a) Red blood cells
    b) White blood cells

c) Platelets
d) Plasma

12. What is the primary function of the small intestine?

    a) Chewing food
    b) Absorbing nutrients
    c) Producing bile
    d) Filtering blood

13. What force keeps the planets in orbit around the Sun?

    a) Magnetism
    b) Friction
    c) Gravity
    d) Tension

14. Which simple machine consists of a wheel with a rope or chain wrapped around it?

    a) Lever
    b) Pulley
    c) Inclined plane
    d) Screw

15. Which of the following materials can be used as an electrical insulator?

    a) Copper
    b) Silver
    c) Glass
    d) Aluminum

16. What is the smallest unit of matter?

   a) Molecule
   b) Atom
   c) Cell
   d) Proton

17. Simple steel is made of two elements—which ones?

   a) Iron and Carbon
   b) Copper and Carbon
   c) Iron and Tin
   d) Iron and Copper

18. What type of bond involves the sharing of electrons between atoms?

   a) Ionic bond
   b) Covalent bond
   c) Hydrogen bond
   d) Metallic bond

19. What is the primary component of magma?

   a) Iron
   b) Water
   c) Molten rock
   d) Carbon dioxide

20. Which type of rock is formed from the cooling and solidification of magma or lava?

   a) Sedimentary rock

BONUS CHAPTER: FAMILY QUIZ & FUN FACTS   171

   b) Metamorphic rock
   c) Igneous rock
   d) Fossiliferous rock

21. When dealing with fossils, excavation is?

   a) The preservation of fossils in sedimentary rock
   b) The process of digging something out
   c) Fossilization
   d) Dating of fossils

How did it go? Here are the Multiple-Choice Answers:

1. b) To detect the environment. Explanation: Sensors are essential for robots to interact with their surroundings, providing data that the robot's controller processes.
2. b) Charles Babbage. Explanation: Charles Babbage is considered the father of the computer for his design of the Analytical Engine.
3. c) Suspension bridge. Explanation: Suspension bridges use cables suspended from towers to support the bridge deck, allowing them to span long distances.
4. c) Chlorophyll. Explanation: Chlorophyll is the pigment in plants that captures light energy for photosynthesis.
5. a) Echolocation. Explanation: Dolphins use echolocation, emitting clicks and listening to the echoes to navigate and hunt.
6. b) Metamorphosis. Explanation: Metamorphosis is the process of transformation from a caterpillar to a butterfly.
7. c) Mars. Explanation: Mars is known as the "Red Planet" due to its iron oxide-rich soil, giving it a reddish appearance.

8. a) Dust and gas. Explanation: A protostar forms from a cloud of dust and gas, which collapses under gravity to start nuclear fusion.
9. a) The point where light cannot escape. Explanation: The event horizon is the boundary around a black hole beyond which no light or other radiation can escape.
10. b) Cerebellum. Explanation: The cerebellum is responsible for coordinating voluntary movements and maintaining balance and posture.
11. c) Platelets. Explanation: Platelets are cell fragments that play a crucial role in blood clotting, helping to prevent excessive bleeding when injuries occur.
12. b) Absorbing nutrients. Explanation: The small intestine's primary function is to absorb nutrients from digested food into the bloodstream.
13. c) Gravity. Explanation: Gravity is the force that keeps the planets in orbit around the Sun, pulling them toward it.
14. b) Pulley. Explanation: A pulley is a simple machine that consists of a wheel with a rope or chain wrapped around it, making it easier to lift heavy objects.
15. c) Glass. Explanation: Glass is an insulator for electricity because its electrons are tightly bonded, so they are not free to move around and conduct electricity.
16. b) Atom. Explanation: Atoms are the smallest units of matter, forming the building blocks of all substances.
17. a) Iron and Carbon. Explanation: Steel is, in its simplest form, an alloy of iron and a few percentages of carbon. It is still one of the world's most important engineering and construction materials.
18. b) Covalent bond. Explanation: Covalent bonds involve the sharing of electrons between atoms, forming molecules like water (H_2O) and carbon dioxide (CO_2).

19. c) Molten rock. Explanation: Magma is primarily composed of molten rock, along with minerals and dissolved gases.
20. c) Igneous rock. Explanation: Igneous rocks form from the cooling and solidification of magma or lava, either beneath the Earth's surface or after volcanic eruptions.
21. b) The process of digging something out. Explanation: Excavation is the careful process of digging up fossils from the ground, using tools and techniques to uncover ancient remains without damaging them. It helps scientists learn about the history of life on Earth.

TRUE OR FALSE—QUIZ

Here are several true or false statements from topics across all fields discussed in this book. You would think that you'd find the pitfalls. But will you?

1. True or False: A robot's power supply is responsible for processing information from its sensors.
2. True or False: The Wright brothers' first powered flight lasted for 12 seconds.
3. True or False: Compression is a force that pulls objects apart.
4. True or False: All plants produce bioluminescence to attract pollinators.
5. True or False: DNA stands for Deoxyribonucleic Acid.
6. True or False: The human brain is made up entirely of muscle tissue.
7. True or False: Jupiter is the smallest planet in our solar system.
8. True or False: A supernova is the explosion of a dying star.

9. True or False: The Milky Way galaxy is the only galaxy in the universe.
10. True or False: The heart is a muscle that pumps blood throughout the body.
11. True or False: The liver produces insulin to regulate blood sugar levels.
12. True or False: The cerebrum is responsible for involuntary actions like breathing and heart rate.
13. True or False: Sound travels faster in air than in water.
14. True or False: A magnet's north pole attracts the north pole of another magnet.
15. True or False: An acid has a pH value greater than 7.
16. True or False: Polymers are made up of long chains of monomers.
17. True or False: In cooking, the Maillard Reaction forces ice to melt.
18. True or False: Glaciers can only form in polar regions.
19. True or False: Earthquakes are caused by the sudden release of energy along fault lines.
20. True or False: All volcanic eruptions are explosive and dangerous.

For sure, that was easy. Here are the correct answers:

1. False. Explanation: The power supply provides energy while the controller processes information from the sensors.
2. True. Explanation: The Wright brothers' first flight in 1903 lasted for 12 seconds, marking a significant milestone in aviation history.
3. False. Explanation: Compression is a force that pushes objects together, not apart.

4. False. Explanation: Not all plants produce bioluminescence; this trait is common in some marine organisms and fungi.
5. True. Explanation: DNA stands for Deoxyribonucleic Acid, the molecule that carries genetic information.
6. False. Explanation: The human brain is primarily composed of neurons, glial cells, and blood vessels, not muscle tissue.
7. False. Explanation: Jupiter is the largest planet in our solar system, not the smallest.
8. True. Explanation: A supernova is indeed the explosive death of a star, resulting in a spectacular burst of light and energy.
9. False. Explanation: The Milky Way is one of billions of galaxies in the universe, each with its own unique characteristics.
10. True. Explanation: The heart is a powerful muscle that continuously pumps blood throughout the body, delivering oxygen and nutrients to cells.
11. False. Explanation: The pancreas, not the liver, produces insulin to regulate blood sugar levels. The liver has many functions, including producing bile for digestion.
12. False. Explanation: The brainstem, not the cerebrum, controls involuntary actions like breathing and heart rate.
13. False. Explanation: Sound travels faster in water than in air because water molecules are closer together, allowing sound waves to travel more quickly.
14. False. Explanation: A magnet's north pole repels the north pole of another magnet, while it attracts the south pole.
15. False. Explanation: An acid has a pH value less than 7, while a base has a pH value greater than 7.
16. True. Explanation: Polymers are indeed made up of long chains of monomers, which can be natural or synthetic.

17. False. Explanation: The Maillard Reaction gives browned foods their distinctive taste and aroma.
18. False. Explanation: Glaciers can form in any region where the accumulation of snow exceeds its melting over time, including high mountain ranges in tropical regions.
19. True. Explanation: Earthquakes are caused by the sudden release of energy along fault lines, resulting from the movement of tectonic plates.
20. False. Explanation: Not all volcanic eruptions are explosive; some are effusive, producing lava flows rather than violent explosions.

A SUMMARY OF FUN FACTS AND TIDBITS

Here is a collection of random fun fact tidbits that you may or may not have encountered by reading the book. Some also complement the topics. Let's do the last science dive of this book:

Robotics and Engineering:

- Charles Babbage designed the Analytical Engine, which laid the groundwork for modern computing, even though it was never completed in his lifetime.
- The Wright brothers' first powered flight in 1903 was just a breakthrough after years of experimentation with their own engine and propellers.
- 3D printing technology is now used to construct bridges, homes, and even body parts, revolutionizing engineering and medical fields.
- The first programmable robot, Unimate, was used on an assembly line in 1961 to lift hot metal pieces, showcasing the beginnings of industrial robotics.

- Modern skyscrapers use tuned mass dampers—giant pendulums inside the building—to reduce the sway caused by wind and earthquakes.

Biology and Life Sciences:

- Dolphins can recognize themselves in mirrors and use unique whistles to identify each other, much like names—all signs of self-awareness.
- The blue whale is the largest animal on Earth, growing up to 100 feet long and weighing as much as 200 tons.
- A single teaspoon of soil can contain over a billion microorganisms, showing how rich and complex life is at the microscopic level.
- Octopuses have three hearts; two pump blood to the gills, and one pumps it to the rest of the body.
- Some species of frogs can freeze solid in the winter and thaw in the spring without suffering any harm.

Astronomy and Space Science:

- Mars has the tallest volcano in the solar system, Olympus Mons, about 13.6 miles high.
- A supernova can outshine an entire galaxy and emit more energy than the Sun will in its entire lifetime.
- The Milky Way galaxy is estimated to contain 100 to 400 billion stars, many of which may have their own planetary systems.
- Astronauts grow taller in space due to the lack of gravity compressing their spine, but they return to their normal height when back on Earth.
- Venus rotates backward compared to most other planets, meaning the Sun rises in the west and sets in the east.

Human Body and Health:

- The cerebellum, a part of the human brain, contains more neurons than the rest of the brain combined despite being much smaller.
- The human heart pumps about five liters or just over one gallon of blood per minute, totaling over 7,000 liters or 2,000 gallons daily.
- If stretched out, the small intestine would be about 20 feet, or six meters, long, providing a large surface area for nutrient absorption.
- Your body produces enough heat in 30 minutes to boil about a liter or 34 ounces of water.
- Fingernails grow faster than toenails, and the nails on your dominant hand grow more quickly than those on your other hand.
- The stomach's lining replaces itself every few days to prevent it from being digested by its own acid.

Physics:

- Pulleys have been used since ancient times, with the earliest known use by the Mesopotamians around 1500 BCE.
- Atoms are mostly empty space. If an atom were the size of a stadium, the nucleus would be the size of a grape.
- Light can travel around the Earth seven and a half times in just one second.
- The speed of sound is slower than the speed of light. That's why you see lightning before hearing thunder.
- The force of gravity on the Moon is only about 1/6th of what it is on Earth, allowing astronauts to take giant leaps.

Chemistry:

- The chemical formula for table salt is NaCl, composed of sodium (Na) and chlorine (Cl) ions.
- Water is the only substance that can exist naturally in all three states of matter—solid, liquid, and gas—on Earth.
- Helium is the second lightest element and is so light that Earth's gravity can't hold on to it, so it escapes into space.
- The bubbles in fizzy drinks are formed by carbon dioxide (CO_2) dissolved under pressure in the liquid.
- The smell of rain comes from a chemical called petrichor, released when rain hits dry soil.

Earth Science and Geology:

- Glaciers hold about 69% of the world's freshwater, acting as giant reservoirs frozen in time.
- The Earth's inner core is as hot as the surface of the Sun, reaching temperatures up to 10,000°F (5,500°C).
- Fossils of plants and animals found on opposite sides of the world are evidence of the ancient supercontinent Pangaea.
- Earthquakes can cause the Earth's surface to shift by several meters in just a few seconds.
- Volcanoes can create new land over time, such as the Hawaiian Islands, which have been formed from volcanic activity over millions of years.
- The Grand Canyon was formed by the erosion caused by the Colorado River over millions of years.

As we've seen, science is a vast field that connects us to the world and the universe in fascinating ways. Stay curious and keep exploring!

REFERENCES

10 natural remedies for a good night's sleep. (2023, August 25). Ploxpop. https://ploxpop.com/web-stories/natural-remedies-for-good-night-sleep/

Astronomical glossary. (n.d.). Caltech. http://ned.ipac.caltech.edu/level5/Glossary/Glossary_M.html

Ayer, D. (2024, February 12). *Can bees cough?* Black Bee Honey. https://blackbeehoney.co/can-bees-cough/

Bartek, M. (2023, November 13). *60 science trivia facts to spark student curiosity.* We Are Teachers. https://www.weareteachers.com/science-trivia-facts/

Benefits of renewable energy use. (2008, July 14). Union of Concerned Scientists. https://www.ucsusa.org/resources/benefits-renewable-energy-use

Best trees to plant in your lawn: A guide for homeowners. (2023, September 11). The Walled Nursery. https://www.thewallednursery.com/best-trees-to-plant-in-your-lawn-a-guide-for-homeowners/

Bioluminescence. (2018, April 30). Smithsonian Ocean. https://ocean.si.edu/ocean-life/fish/bioluminescence

Blood circulation. (n.d.). AimHigh! https://aimhigh.space/transport-system-in-humans/blood-circulation/

Bosman, A. (2022, April 1). *Complete sequencing of the human genome reveals new findings.* Earth.Com. https://www.earth.com/news/complete-sequencing-of-the-human-genome-reveals-new-findings/

Brain anatomy and how the brain works. (2021, July 14). Johns Hopkins Medicine. https://www.hopkinsmedicine.org/health/conditions-and-diseases/anatomy-of-the-brain

Bridge | history, design, types, parts, & facts. (n.d.). Encyclopaedia Britannica. https://www.britannica.com/technology/bridge-engineering

Bromley, A. G. (1998). Charles Babbage's Analytical Engine, 1838. *IEEE Annals of the History of Computing, 20*(4), 29–45. https://web.archive.org/web/20160304081812id_/http://profs.scienze.univr.it/~manca/storia-informatica/babbage.pdf

Charlotte, E. (2023, December 18). Discovering the enchanting world of stars: A journey through space. *SRUNE.* https://srune.com/stars/

Children's misconceptions about science. (n.d.). Clayton School District. https://www.claytonschools.net/cms/lib/MO01000419/Centricity/Domain/442/Childrens_Misconception.pdf

182 REFERENCES

Circulation of blood through the heart. (n.d.). MedlinePlus. https://medlineplus.gov/ency/imagepages/19387.htm

Conzemius, E. (2023, March 2). *Types of planets in astronomy.* Astronomypr.Com. https://www.astronomypr.com/types-of-planets-in-astronomy

Daniel. (2024, January 4). Bones and joints: A 3D exploration of the skeletal system. *Doctors Digest.* https://doctorsdigest.net/bones-and-joints-a-3d-exploration-of-the-skeletal-system/

Demystifying electromagnetism: Definition, examples, and facts. (2023, July 10). *Free Science Information.* https://freescience.info/demystifying-electromagnetism-definition-examples-and-facts/

DeVille, K. (2024, March 25). *10 most amazing facts about space—Stem education guide.* STEM Education Guide. https://stemeducationguide.com/amazing-facts-about-space/

Direct imaging—Exoplanets. (2018, January 20). University of Geneva. https://www.unige.ch/sciences/astro/exoplanets/en/research/direct-imaging

Electricity: The basics. (n.d.). *NYU ITP Physical Computing.* https://itp.nyu.edu/physcomp/lessons/electronics/electricity-the-basics/

Electromagnetism guide for KS3 physics students. (n.d.). BBC Bitesize. https://www.bbc.co.uk/bitesize/articles/z7922v4

Engineering: Simple machines—lesson. (n.d.). TeachEngineering.Org. https://www.teachengineering.org/lessons/view/cub_simple_lesson01

Exoplanets. (n.d.). NASA. https://science.nasa.gov/exoplanets/

Fossel, M. B. (2004). *Cells, aging, and human disease* (1st ed.). Oxford University Press.

Fumagalli, G. (2022, January 3). *The disappearance of glaciers is changing the face of our planet.* Treedom. https://blog.treedom.net/en/the-disappearance-of-glaciers-is-changing-the-face-of-our-planet

Galileo's leaning tower of Pisa experiment. (2024). In *Wikipedia.* https://en.wikipedia.org/w/index.php?title=Galileo%27s_Leaning_Tower_of_Pisa_experiment&oldid=1244751795

Galileo's leaning tower of Pisa experiment overturned a theory of which ancient Greek scientist? (2023, September 21). Rise of Kingdoms Answers. https://rokanswers.com/galileos-leaning-tower-of-pisa-experiment-overturned-a-theory-of-which-ancient-greek-scientist/

Graham, A. (2022, July 14). Four ways to drastically reduce infections in your home. *Tempo Stand.* https://tempostand.com/reducing-bacterial-and-viral-infections-at-home/

Harness, J. (2023, September 28). Difference between meteor vs asteroid. *HowWhichWhy.* https://howwhichwhy.com/difference-between-meteor-vs-asteroid/

Harris, T., & Pollette, C. (2022, January 10). *How robots work*. HowStuffWorks. https://science.howstuffworks.com/robot.htm

Helmenstine, Anne Marie. (2020, February 3). *Why the periodic table is important*. ThoughtCo. https://www.thoughtco.com/why-is-the-periodic-table-important-608829

Helmenstine, A. M. (2024, May 11). *Examples of chemical reactions taking place around you every day*. ThoughtCo. https://www.thoughtco.com/examples-of-chemical-reactions-in-everyday-life-604049

Herbst, C. (2023, March 15). 100+ science trivia questions for kids (2024). *Milwaukee With Kids*. https://www.mkewithkids.com/post/science-trivia-questions-for-kids/

Hill, K. (2010, July 30). *How hot is the planet Venus and why is Venus known as the hottest planet in the solar system?* Zippy Facts. https://zippyfacts.com/how-hot-is-the-planet-venus-and-why-is-venus-known-as-the-hottest-planet-in-the-solar-system/

Household items as pH indicators. (2023, October). University of Tennessee Institute of Agriculture. https://utia.tennessee.edu/publications/wp-content/uploads/sites/269/2023/10/W925.pdf

How many types of volcanoes are there? 3, 4, 5, or 6. (2023, February 25). MidGeo. https://midgeo.com/how-many-types-of-volcanoes-are-there/

How the immune system protects you from infection. (n.d.). Pfizer. https://www.pfizer.com/news/articles/how_the_immune_system_protects_you_from_infection

Human bones facts—Human body. (2018, January 12). Cool Kid Facts. https://www.coolkidfacts.com/human-bones-facts/

In the loop. (2023, April 13). Smore. https://secure.smore.com/n/k5gfs-in-the-loop

Irving, M. (2019, August 15). *Virtual universes study suggests habitable Earth-like exoplanets are more common than we thought*. New Atlas. https://newatlas.com/habitable-earthlike-exoplanets-estimate/61066/

Jaggard, V. (2019, June 15). *Phases of the moon, explained*. National Geographic. https://www.nationalgeographic.com/science/article/full-moon

Jakubowska, J. (2008, November 11). *Genome Visualisation and User Studies in Biologist-Computer Interaction*. University of Glasgow. https://core.ac.uk/download/293036394.pdf

Kamara, K. (n.d.). *How does a dolphin echolocate?* Woods Hole Oceanographic Institution. https://www.whoi.edu/science/B/people/kamara/echolocation.html

Łasiński, D. (2024, September 18). *Unlocking the secrets to deep sleep: Strategies for restful nights*. Pyrilia. https://www.pyrilia.com/blog/unlocking-secrets-deep-sleep

184 REFERENCES

Law of conservation of mass. (n.d.). *eTutorWorld*. https://www.etutorworld.com/7th-grade-science-worksheets/law-of-conservation-of-mass.html

Lisa. (2024, May 14). The science of sound for kids: Exploring the basics of acoustics. *ABF Creative*. https://www.abfc.co/the-science-of-sound-for-kids-exploring-the-basics-of-acoustics/

Lizard—Facts, size, diet, pictures. (2023, May 17). All Animal Facts. https://allanimalfacts.com/lizard/

Mather, R. (2022). Revolutionizing astronomy and astrophysics: The exploration and study of exoplanets. *Journal of Science and Geosciences, 10*(4), 7–7. https://doi.org/10.51268/2736-187X.22.10.85

Menon, S. (2024, February 27). Top 10 animals with unique adaptations. *Smore Science Magazine*. https://www.smorescience.com/top-10-animals-with-unique-adaptations/

Miner, J. (2023, May 6). How far will bees travel from the hive? *BeeKeepinglove.Com*. https://beekeepinglove.com/how-far-will-bees-travel-from-the-hive

Morgan, A. (2024, February 8). Can animals talk to each other? *Online Field Guide*. https://www.online-field-guide.com/can-animals-talk-to-each-other/

Mount St Helens. (2023, November 11). Vajiram & Ravi. https://vajiramandravi.com/

Muskopf, S. (2019, April 5). Digestive concept map. *The Biology Corner*. https://www.biologycorner.com/2019/04/05/digestive-concept-map/

Newton's law of universal gravitation facts for kids. (n.d.). Kiddle. https://kids.kiddle.co/Newton%27s_law_of_universal_gravitation

Optics: Light, color, and their uses educator guide. (n.d.). NASA. https://www.nasa.gov/stem-content/optics-light-color-and-their-uses-educator-guide/

Paige, A. (2024, August 22). *60 Powerful education quotes for kids [2024 Updated list]*. SplashLearn Blog – Educational Resources for Parents, Teachers & Kids. https://www.splashlearn.com/blog/powerful-education-quotes-for-kids-to-realize-the-importance-of-learning/

Pattis, R. E. (1981). *Karel the robot: A gentle introduction to the art of programming*. https://compedu.stanford.edu/karel-reader/docs/python/en/chapter1.html

Photosynthesis review. (n.d.). Khan Academy. https://www.khanacademy.org/science/ap-biology/cellular-energetics/photosynthesis/a/hs-photosynthesis-review

Planets (10 questions). (n.d.). Trivia Quiz Uk. https://quiz.uk/planets-10-questions/

poojashgwn@gmail.com. (2023, August 27). What is Bioluminescence? *My Wildlife World*. https://kingwildlife.com/what-is-bioluminescence/

Reyes, J. M. (2024, January 9). How do black holes work? *ESTEEMStream.News*. https://esteemstream.news/91133/transportation/space/how-do-black-holes-work/

Robinson, K., Watchon, M., & Laird, A. (2020). *Aberrant cerebellar circuitry in the spinocerebellar ataxias*. Frontiers in Neuroscience.

School physics quiz: Light—Multiple choice. (n.d.). Syvum. https://www.syvum.com/cgi/online/mult.cgi/squizzes/physics/light.tdf

Science for kids: The atom. (n.d.). Ducksters. https://www.ducksters.com/science/the_atom.php

Simple science activities. (n.d.). PBS KIDS for Parents. https://www.pbs.org/parents/simple-science-activities

Sofia, L. (2023, October 4). *The fascinating facts of rocketry: Unveiling the marvels of space exploration*. https://www.lolaapp.com/facts-about-the-rocket/

Solar system exploration program. (n.d.). NASA. https://www.nasa.gov/planetarymissions/solar-system-exploration-program/

Structure of the atom. (n.d.). SliderBase. https://www.sliderbase.com/spitem-1119-4.html

Studying for the social work exam. (2012, December 13). Social Work Test Prep. https://socialworktestprep.com/blog/2012/december/13/studying-for-the-social-work-exam/

The great 1906 San Francisco earthquake. (n.d.). USGS. https://earthquake.usgs.gov/earthquakes/events/1906calif/18april/

The Life Cycles of Stars: How Supernovae Are Formed. (n.d.). NASA Goddard Space Flight Center. https://imagine.gsfc.nasa.gov/educators/lessons/xray_spectra/background-lifecycles.html

The rock cycle. (n.d.). National Geographic. https://education.nationalgeographic.org/resource/rock-cycle

The wonders of water: How is this chemical the key to life? (2016, March 22). How It Works. https://www.howitworksdaily.com/the-wonders-of-water-how-is-this-chemical-the-key-to-life/

Tiwari, S. (2023, July 17). *Exploring bioluminescence: From deep-sea creatures to glowing mushrooms*. News Track. https://english.newstracklive.com/news/exploring-bioluminescence-from-deepsea-creatures-to-glowing-mushrooms-emc-sc54-nu384-ta384-1285304-1.html

Top 7 application of computer in science. (2024, February 6). *Concepts All*. https://conceptsall.com/application-of-computer-in-science/

Top 10 amazing facts about the sun! (2023, April 19). *Gkbooks*. https://gkbooks.in/web-stories/top-10-interesting-facts-about-the-sun-gk-facts-you-need-to-know/

Volcanoes: Principal types of volcanoes. (n.d.). USGS. https://pubs.usgs.gov/gip/volc/types.html

Ward, C. (2024, January 16). *Astronomers find a planet half-covered in lava*. SYFY

186   REFERENCES

Official Site. https://www.syfy.com/syfy-wire/astronomers-find-a-planet-half-covered-in-lava

What's the difference between high tide and low tide? (2023, September 6). Difference Digest. https://differencedigest.com/nature/whats-the-difference-between-high-tide-and-low-tide/

Williamson, T. (2021, December 1). *History of computers: A brief timeline.* Livescience.Com. https://www.livescience.com/20718-computer-history.html

YMCA L2 anatomy—Circulatory system. (2023, March 15). ProProfs. https://www.proprofs.com/quiz-school/story.php?title=mjewnzk3oqzzb7

Your digestive system & how it works. (n.d.). National Institute of Diabetes and Digestive and Kidney Diseases. https://www.niddk.nih.gov/health-information/digestive-diseases/digestive-system-how-it-works

IMAGE REFERENCES

If not mentioned otherwise, the publisher of this book used propitiatory images, acquired image licenses, or used artificial intelligence to generate basic images and has modified them in every case with human design craft to suit the purpose or remove factually incorrect details. While images created through artificial intelligence are understandably not copyrighted, most of such pictures in this book have received significant manual human editing. Please, therefore, contact the publisher for any commercial re-use of illustrations from this book. Use for private and non-commercial educational purposes is, of course, not only granted but welcome.

The following images, however, are based on the listed references. We appreciate the sources who provided the free licenses enabling us to create this great content and the designers and authors involved in the background.

"DNA double helix" is a modified image of: Servier Medical Art. (2023). DNA. https://smart.servier.com/smart_image/dna/

"Solar System Planetary System" is a modified image of: Pixabay. (2021). Space Solar System Galaxy Universe. https://pixabay.com/photos/space-solar-system-galaxy-universe-6476289/

"Moon phases" is a modified image of: NASA. (2023). Moon Phases. https://science.nasa.gov/moon/moon-phases/

"Eclipses" is a modified image of: Vecteezy. (n.d.). Diagram Showing Eclipses with Sun and Earth. https://www.vecteezy.com/vector-art/1130700-diagram-showing-eclipses-with-sun-and-earth

"Human Brain Anatomy vector graphic" is a modified version of: Pixabay. (2013).

Brain Human Anatomy Organ. https://pixabay.com/vectors/brain-human-anatomy-organ-medicine-148131/

"Human bone joints" is an extraction from: Servier Medical Art. (2023). Bones. https://smart.servier.com/wp-content/uploads/2016/10/Bones.pptx

"MODEL OF A LITHIUM ATOM" is a modified version of: Pixabay. (2017). Lithium Atom Isolated Atomic. https://pixabay.com/illustrations/lithium-atom-isolated-atomic-2784853/

"Volcano Types" is a modified version of: Vecteezy. (n.d.). Volcano Vectors. https://www.vecteezy.com/vector-art/8554125-volcano-vector-set-collection-graphic-clipart-design

Printed in Great Britain
by Amazon